all
about THEATRE

all about
THEATRE

Derek Bowskill

W. H. Allen · London and New York · 1975

(A division of Howard & Wyndham Ltd)

Copyright © 1975 by Derek Bowskill

Set in Monotype Times 11 on 13 pt.
and printed in Great Britain by
Richard Clay (The Chaucer Press) Ltd
Bungay Suffolk
for the publishers
W. H. Allen & Co. Ltd.,
44 Hill Street, London W1X 8LB

ISBN 0 491 01815 0

CONTENTS

For the Multi Media Wizard of
One Man Theatre, Ron Geesin:
with affection for him
and his friendly family.

PREFACE

THE AIM OF THIS BOOK IS TO
show how the theatre works today, rather than to describe
its past—although its history is not overlooked.

Undoubtedly the best way to learn about drama is to see
plays in action, in front of an audience, where their theatrical
qualities may be enjoyed . . . and later, to read them in peace
and quiet at home so their literary qualities can be appreciated.

An important feature of this book, stressing the importance of the here-and-now of theatre, is the special considera-
tion given in Chapter 7 to the making of the first production
of *Life Class*. I would like to take this opportunity of thanking
all those concerned with the play for their generous help
while I constantly questioned them. I hope my report does
not misrepresent them and does them full justice. Certainly,
my book would be the poorer without their contributions.

This book will help you understand something of the many
preparations that occur before a made-up actor appears,
costumed and lit, on a stage in front of an audience. It will
also help you understand some of the challenges and problems that face a playwright. The elements concerned in these
different aspects of making a play (the live performance by
actors and the playwright's script) are the two major factors

in the workings of the theatre and I hope this book will
encourage you to get involved with them yourself: watching
plays and making and presenting them; namely, in what the
theatre is all about.

DEREK BOWSKILL

FOREWORD

PROFESSIONALS ARE OFTEN SUS-
picious, if not actually scornful, of books with titles like *All
About Theatre*. Sometimes they are right. There can be no
such thing as an 'All' where the theatre or any other art is
concerned. What there can be is a concise statement of
essentials, a viewpoint from which the subject can begin to
be correctly surveyed. That is what this book, quite exception-
ally, provides.

The theatre is above all the place for learning by experience. There are acting schools of course, and colleges of
design: but the best lessons are learned by practice. And for
directors there seems to be no other way. This makes a clear
and uncluttered introduction like Derek Bowskill's all the
more valuable. Here is a writer, clearly, with practical experience of his own. This must be why his pages are so freshly
clear of prejudice and pedagogy.

Naturally I personally have found Mr Bowskill's observations on the production of *Life Class* particularly interesting:
it is always surprising (and sometimes salutary) to see ourselves as others see us. In fact, though, I find that Derek
Bowskill has understood and described my principles of
production—which I have never formulated myself—with
extraordinary accuracy as well as with the most sympathetic
perception.

I would only add one warning. These principles (which of course I believe in) are not very common in the professional theatre. They demand qualities like mutual respect, individual responsibility and whole-hearted commitment which have little to do with conventional professionalism, and nothing to do with egotistical careerism. Contrary to what many people believe, such qualities are wonderfully common among actors. Opportunism and lack of scruple are common enough in the theatrical profession: but actors will almost always respond to a sincerely creative lead. Bless them.

LINDSAY ANDERSON

1 DRAMA IN THE BEGINNING

GOING TO THE THEATRE IS EASY.
All you have to do is choose a theatre, go to the box-office and pay for a ticket. Sometimes you may need to book in advance, but generally you will be able to arrive on chance and walk straight in. You will be shown to your seat. You will sit down and wait for the play to begin.

But what kind of play will it be: comedy, tragedy, farce or thriller? Will it include music, song and dance? Will the stage be at one end of a long hall hidden behind curtains, on an open platform across one end, in the middle of the floor in a circle or a square, or will the actors wander all over the place? Will the production be simple or sophisticated: will the actors appear in strange make-up and unlikely clothes, will film and television play a part, will there be a lot of sound and light effects? And what about you? Will you just sit down and look at a stage a long way from you, or will you be so close that you could reach out and touch the actors? Will you become involved emotionally, or even physically, in what is happening?

No matter what the answers to these questions, the chances are that it will take place in a special building, at a special time, and that you will have to pay to see it. But things have not always been that way. Drama has not always been plays,

and plays have not always taken place in theatres. So, to
begin at the beginning, what are plays, what is drama and
what is theatre all about?

In *Chambers Twentieth Century Dictionary* it says that
drama comes from a Greek word meaning 'to do'. Its defini-
tion reads: 'a story of life and action for representation by
actors'. **Theatre** is defined as a 'scene of action, field of
operations: the stage: an audience, house: the drama: a body
of plays'. It is true that drama and theatre have been in-
fluenced by the Greeks, but their real beginnings came
thousands of years before, when man first became aware of
the precarious nature of his life and his surroundings.

Drama is basically about the communication of thoughts
and feelings between people. The main differences between
drama and theatre are that drama involves small numbers of
people who all take part in an event that can come to life at
almost any time, anywhere, while **theatre** involves large
numbers, divided into those who watch and those who act,
and happens in set places at set times. Drama is an act, theatre
is a ritual, and primitive **ritual** is how it all started.

Man looked around for some way of controlling his life
and his destiny. He thought that just as he hunted and tamed
inferior animals, so some god was hunting and taming him.
Man knew he succeeded best with wild animals by dressing
up in their skins and wearing masks, so he thought he could
best influence his god by dressing up like him. Since he had
no idea of what this god looked like he imagined him to be a
magnification of all his own joys and fears and dressed in
different ways to express these feelings.

Now primitive man did not know the universe very well.
There were few things he could understand or control. (You
have only to think about the rising and setting of the sun or
the night sky to share something of primitive man's wonder.)

Primitive rituals performed by early man

He was preoccupied mainly by birth and death, the sun, moon and stars, the weather and the changing seasons. Primitive man felt there was a god somewhere with a set of rules that controlled him and his world. He dressed up like his god to please him, and he invented rules he thought were like his god's. These rules told him how to parade to influence his god and they were handed down from generation to generation. Over the years they grew into ritual and often came to be associated with magic or religion.

The Druids with their knives and dances at Stonehenge perhaps, and the North American Indians with their feathers and painted bodies are just two examples.

The rituals consisted of dressing-up, song and dance. The song was mainly chanting and howling since words were few, and the dance was very basic, mainly running, squatting and jumping up and down.

The dressing-up in clothes, masks and make-up was not only intended to please the gods but also to protect the human being underneath so that if anything went wrong the god could be blamed, so releasing the impersonator from danger. Even today, whenever one of us has to act in any special manner, we often use uniforms, make-up and masks to help in one way or another. (Think of the occasions and activities for which people wear special clothes, especially masks, and decide for yourself how valid the idea is.) So the dressed-up human appeared as a god, and in song and dance he publicly paraded, proclaimed and celebrated his joys and fears. These three elements—parading, proclaiming and celebrating—have always been important ingredients in drama and theatre.

2 THE STORY OF THE THEATRE

THIS BOOK IS MAINLY ABOUT drama today, what is happening in the theatre here and now, and this can best be understood by looking at the way it has grown from its earliest days. A brief look back helps us place today's theatre at the end of a direct development over approximately five thousand years. When considered country by country, this development is difficult to follow since there are often local, confusing features. When looked at world-wide, however, it can be seen to be as straight as a die.

The first religious rituals that we can recognize as fore-runners of classical Greek drama were those of the Egyptians. In the years 3000 to 2000 B.C. there was a regular event (it is difficult to know whether to call it a production, a festival, a service or a happening with the audience taking part) that we now call the **Abydos Passion Play**. It certainly contained many elements of celebration and, in its ritualistic way, told the story of the death of Osiris and how his limbs were pulled off and torn apart, to be rejoined and healed by his sister-wife, Isis. There is little doubt there was some dramatic portrayal, but there was also the actual sacrificial slaughter of the many living slaves who died from the tearing-off of the limbs. This real and bloody participation separates the Abydos Passion Play from ordinary plays, but the important

Chinese make-up derived from a mask

elements were there, and they formed the basis for the first of the three main ingredients of theatre: **ritual**.

The second of the main ingredients was provided by the Chinese Theatre about 1,000 years later. This was the **lyrical** element, and it showed itself in Chinese Theatre in the form of stylized song. Chinese plays were more like operas than any other form of theatre, combining, as they did, long passages of chanting with insistently loud music. Although there was some use of natural voice and speech, the lion's share of all the plays went to the lyrical sections with their music.

The third and last of the main ingredients came from the Indian Theatre of about the same period. Insistently loud music was an accompaniment here too, not for the lyrical element of song but for the mimicry of stylized **dance** that was a major feature of Indian Theatre. Costume and make-up were equally stylized, not so much to assist dramatic characterization, but to help the expression of delicate movements and gestures of head, eyes and eyelids, lips and tongue and fingers and toes. It is true that there was some spoken dialogue, but it was secondary to the mimic sections with their music.

The Greeks are often called the fathers of modern drama. To do them justice their real contribution was not to create anything new and original but to combine what had been separate paths—in Egypt, China and India—into the one broad highway that was to lead to Western drama and theatre as we now know it.

The trend started about 700 B.C. and was given its shape by **Aeschylus** and those who came after him about 200 years later. They combined the previously separate elements of religious ritual, mimic dance and lyric song (all with their supporting music) into a new unity: dramatic theatre.

Their earliest plays presented man as a pawn in the hands

Greek theatre in action

of powerful gods. As the plays developed, man began to
emerge as a being in charge of his future, aware and responsible, perceptive and responsive. While at first they were little
more than sophisticated versions of the primitive view, they
gradually began to take the more civilized outlook that the
proper subject of any play is man himself.

As was mentioned in Chapter 1, the Greeks gave us
the word 'drama' meaning 'to do'. They also gave us two
other important words and ideas: **tragedy** (the old Greek
word for the cry of a goat at the time of its slaughter), being a
play with an unhappy ending; and **comedy** (originally meaning a revel or orgy), being a play of humour and, more often

than not, of hope. This is, however, to oversimplify and we shall look at these ideas again more closely.

At its best, Greek drama has not yet been surpassed, and after it there was only one way the theatre could go and that was 'down. The decline started with the fall of Athens, continued during the rise and fall of the Roman Empire, with brief spasms of inspiration from extremist writers and comic mimes, and touched bottom during the Dark Ages.

Theatre in England began where the Greeks had started, through a representation of man dwarfed by comparison with his master, in this case the Christian God.

Historically there is a gap, but dramatically none at all. The Greek stage was a temple and the actors were priests. The beginnings were similar in England. There was a fully formed version of a play performed all over Europe between A.D. 900 and 1400, generally known as the **Quem Quaeritis** from one of its very few lines: 'Quem quaeritis in sepulchro, O Christicolae?' ('Whom do ye seek in the sepulchre, O Christian women?'). The stage was in a church near the altar, and the characters (the three Marys and an angel) were portrayed by priests.

This dramatic and religious ritual was how the theatre began in England. It soon grew into the four main types of medieval drama: the **mystery**—an extension in dramatic form of Christian ritual; the **miracle**—the acts and miracles of the saints of the Church; the **morality**—representations of Good and Evil as they struggled for the soul of man; and the **interlude**—a light-hearted piece between two major plays, or parts of a play. The morality play set out to improve its audience while the interlude attempted to entertain it.

The last two started the move away from the Church as the only stage and Latin as the only language. Plays in English came out into the open. All four types had three important things in common: a mixing and mingling of actors and audience, a number of platforms or areas set aside always to represent *special* places and the space in between them representing anywhere else.

Moralities and Interludes were naturals to start the theatre touring. The plays appealed to the people and they were easy to take on tour, requiring only a small cast and a handful of props. They had flexible scripts and the actors could perform all the tricks of acrobats, jugglers and clowns. The travelling groups performed on village greens, inn-yards, moot-halls and churches, and could always turn to the near-by Great House expecting a welcome, food, shelter and a chance to be paid to perform, provided they presented the kind of play the host wanted. So, perhaps, began the tradition: 'For we that live to please, must please to live', and the theatre came to life again.

To understand how the theatre came to flourish in the time of Elizabeth I we must consider a rather special marriage that took place around about that time. On one side was the native British flair for compromise and survival, with the love of language inherited from the Church services, the mysteries and other plays mentioned above and the passion for rhetoric which governed language in England at the time. On the other side was the Latin flair for the flashy life-style of the **commedia dell'arte**, travelling professionals who specialized in spontaneity and alertness combined with dazzling physical prowess and a cheeky common touch. The marriage was successful and its best-known result was William Shakespeare.

Shakespeare moved the English nation, from its queen to its beggars, and spoke to his countrymen in language they liked and understood about things of moral, social and political importance. This was no mean feat and his words still jump in our ears and excite our minds three centuries later. In Shakespeare's hands tragedy became a sensitive examination of human beings against a backcloth of eternity; comedy became a keen exposure of people's weaknesses and conceits as they played the games that only people can play; and tragi-comedy blended the two, with humour and hope striving to discover beauty and truth in sad stories of blemished human beings.

It took five hundred years to create Shakespeare, his Playhouse and all it stood for, but less than fifty to cripple it. The apparent culprit was the Plague, but it was the finger of Puritanism that put the writing on the wall. The text ran: 'Whereas the distressed Estate of Ireland, steeped in her own Blood, and the distracted Estate of England, threatened with a cloud of Blood, by a Civill Warre, call for all possible meanes to appease and avert the Wrath of God appearing in these Judgements; among which Fasting and Prayer have been often tried to be very effectual, have been lately, and are still enjoyned, and whereas publicke Sports doe not well agree with publicke Calamities, nor publicke Stage-playes with the seasons of Humiliation, this being an exercise of sad and pious solemnity and the other being Spectacles too commonly expressing lascivious Mirth and Levitie. It is therefore thought fit, and Ordeined by the Lords and Commons in this Parliament Assembled, that while these sad Causes and set times of Humiliation doe continue, publicke Stage-Playes shall cease, and bee foreborne. Instead of which are recommended to the people of this Land, the profitable and season-able Considerations of Repentance, Reconciliation, and peace with God, which probably may produce outward peace and prosperity, and bring again Times of Joy and Gladness to these Nations.'

For the rest of the century few playhouses were open, and they became less platforms for plays than meeting houses for aristocratic men-about-town and their ladies and hangers-on. The play was no longer the important thing and tragedy became sensation; comedy became farce; and tragi-comedy, perhaps Shakespeare's greatest gift to the theatre, became mere sentiment before it finally passed away. A fitting tribute to the times came at the end of the seventeenth century with Congreve's *Way of the World*.

In 1713 came more writing on the wall and also in an Official Act: 'For reducing the laws relating to rogues, vagabonds, sturdy beggars and vagrants, and sending them whither they ought to be sent.' Under the Act, 'Common players of Interludes' were 'rogues and vagabonds'. In spite of this Act, or perhaps because of it, John Gay's *Beggar's Opera* took London by storm and could have been the herald of a rebirth of lusty theatre. It was after all the source of inspiration for Bertolt Brecht and Kurt Weill to create *Die Dreigröschenoper* years later, but any such hope for the English Theatre was nipped in the bud by yet another Act. This time the text proclaimed that any player acting 'for hire, gain or reward . . . without licence from the Lord Chamberlain of His Majesty's Household for the time being, shall be deemed a rogue and vagabond'.

In spite of the attitudes and opinions of the times, Goldsmith and Sheridan tried to stem the flow of sentiment and one of the special aspects of their genius was that they were great in spite of their times.

Melodrama and sentiment gradually took over and gained such a hold that even the combined onslaught of such writers as Zola, Ibsen and Strindberg, with the support of the critic William Archer and the talent of George Bernard Shaw, was not enough to shift hypocrisy and sentiment from their commanding positions in the English theatre. It was to take two world wars and the resulting social upheaval before three crucial plays burst into the English arena. They all enjoyed considerable success in their different spheres of influence and all three brought substantial changes in their wake.

Look Back in Anger, by John Osborne, was first performed in London on 8 May 1956. It was hailed as a landmark in the modern theatre. In fact, its impact and importance were more social than dramatic. What happened was that a writer achieved a success with a play that moved away from the drawing-rooms of the upper middle-class to the living areas of the lower middle-class. This was a social landmark.

The dramatic landmarks came in 1958 with *The Sport of My Mad Mother*, by Ann Jellicoe, and in 1959 with *Sergeant Musgrave's Dance*, by John Arden.

Arden and Jellicoe succeeded where other considerable talents had failed. These two writers created a significant and imaginative trend for the twentieth century. They would not have succeeded, however, unless the ground had been well prepared by Beckett, Brecht and Genet, who were in their own way all products of the same kind of marriage that had created Shakespeare and his theatre all those years before.

These writers freed the theatre from its 300-years-old shackles and the new plays that followed demanded new stage shapes, new actors and new relationships with their audiences, new production techniques and new attitudes to the theatre. The unexpected had happened, and England, after three centuries in the theatrical doldrums, built new theatres for old, and in the time of Elizabeth II became again what it had been in the time of Elizabeth I, the living heart of world theatre.

In the preface to the new version of *The Sport of My Mad Mother*, Ann Jellicoe writes about her play and the theatre at large. What she has to say is an excellent bridge between this brief story of the theatre and the next chapter, which examines the different components that make a play.

'*The Sport of My Mad Mother* was not written intellectually according to a prearranged plan. It was shaped bit by bit until the bits felt right in relation to each other and to the whole. It is an anti-intellect play not only because it is about irrational forces and urges but because one hopes it will reach the audience directly through rhythm, noise and music and their reaction to basic stimuli.

'The play is written to be acted: nothing is put in words that cannot be shown in action. Very often the words counterpoint the action or intensify the action by conflicting with it. Most of the people in the play distrust emotion and haven't the means to express it anyway and they tend to say things which they think will sound good. But at the same time they betray their real feeling either by what they do, or by the very fact that they need to assume a mask.

'It has taken me some years to understand that the play is based upon myth and uses ritual. Myth is the bodying forth in images and stories of our deepest fears and conflicts. *The Sport of My Mad Mother* is concerned with fear and rage at being rejected . . .

'We create rituals when we want to strengthen, celebrate or define our common life and common values, or when we want to give ourselves confidence to undertake a common course of action. A ritual generally takes the form of repeating a pattern of words and gestures which tend to excite us above a normal state of mind; at the climax of the rite the essential nature of something is changed (e.g. the mass, a marriage service, the bestowal of diplomas, etc.).'

3 WHAT MAKES A PLAY

IT WAS SUGGESTED IN THE previous chapter that the combination of ritual, lyric and mimicry made the stuff of drama. From the performer's point of view, all these come from the text from which he works—the script from which he takes his words and actions in the first place. But a play only comes fully to life when it is shared with an audience. Then, and only then, does drama become an act of theatre. For this act of theatre to work, the audience must be willing to accept a 'let's pretend' situation, or what has been called the 'willing suspension of disbelief'.

Drama and theatre are works of art. This does not mean they have to be mustily cultural or boringly impressive. It merely means they appeal to the imagination. It means they concern themselves with exposing and illuminating reality, not creating it. Take the case of a football match. You can watch recordings on television, examine the results tables or read a comprehensive and no doubt exciting report on the sports page. None of these ways of telling what happened is dramatic. But when one man in a pub says to another: 'Look, you be the winger and I'll be the back. There's the ball. Now it happened like this . . .'—then the replay, the 'Let's Pretend' re-telling, becomes dramatic. One man is going to pretend to be somebody else and those watching are going to encourage him. They will *take part* in the pretence in fact. Without such co-operation from an audience no performance stands a chance of dramatic effect.

The audience's willingness to play a game of 'Let's Pretend' depends on many different factors. One of these is the way the actors have been equipped to take their part in the performance. It was suggested in Chapter 1 that drama was life and action as represented by actors. This, more often than not, means speaking and moving, so it is essential that the audience should be able to see what is happening and hear what is being said. This may appear to be obvious, but there are many actors and directors who appear not to accept it. If you find this difficult to believe, listen carefully the next time you go to the theatre, and see how often a member of the audience says to his neighbour 'What did he say?' or 'I couldn't hear so-and-so'.

The actors, then, must be seen and heard; but seen and heard doing what? Well, probably a play written to be performed on the stage. The Italian commedia dell'arte of centuries ago, the variety artists and market-stall holders of today and many pub and club entertainers all have in common an ability to hold the attention of an audience without a scripted text. But when performances involve many actors and last for up to three hours, they will have had some kind of text suggesting, if not actually telling, what they should do and say. It is also likely that they will have needed a lengthy rehearsal period to memorize the text and practise the action. The writer must put into his play enough information for the actors and the director to understand what he is getting at and how he intends them to communicate it to an audience.

The question of communication is one of the most important aspects of the work of everyone concerned in the theatre. It is also crucial to the audience. It is above all vital to the actor. He performs with his body and voice, making the character come alive and walk and talk.

First, let us consider how he must be able to use his voice. At the lowest level he must be heard and understood by every member of the audience. This means simple, straightforward, clear speech.

Good speech captures the interest of the listener straightaway. It commands attention not by shouting, ranting and raving (these can be used to good effect from time to time, but can soon become boring and irritating), but simply by being good speech. Not only does it catch the attention, it does so to good effect since it can be easily understood, and so make even the most complicated ideas seem simple, which is important in the theatre since many playwrights can be complex and obscure. Good speech in the theatre makes for efficiency and courtesy, and audiences are always impressed when they feel the actors are considering their needs.

No actor can afford to possess a speech defect or voice mannerism, since these will come between him and his audience, and people will listen for his peculiarities and not to what he is saying. This is not to suggest that an actor should not use special voices and styles of speech when he is playing a character, as this is part of his job. For example, *Riders to the Sea* is set in Ireland and *Hobson's Choice* in the North of England: both plays need appropriate accents. An actor should aim at all times for a variety and flexibility of voice and speech that suit the role he is taking and help the understanding of the audience.

'It's not what you say, but the way that you say it' is a well-known phrase from a well-worn song, but it still contains an important truth that no actor can afford to overlook. No matter how beautiful his voice or brilliant his speech, they will avail him little unless they are accurately put to work in the service of the play as a whole and the actor's individual part in it.

One of the most important factors in helping an actor achieve good voice and speech in his performances is his **breathing**. Inhalation and exhalation, the whole process of respiration, depend upon movement. The muscles of the diaphragm and those between the ribs contract and relax to provide the regular intake and expulsion of air that make up normal breathing. Most breathing is natural and unconscious and in everyday life deep and correct breathing can promote good posture and keep the body generally in good tone. It can also help build up powers of concentration, a factor invaluable to an actor.

In addition to the normal breathing requirements of everyday life, an actor has two special needs. First, his speech and voice must always be under full control since no actor can hope to give a decent performance if he is out of breath. Second, the athletic demands of his profession may call upon him to use the energies and disciplines of a professional football player or dancer. It is these demands, namely **movement** and **gesture** that we now turn to.

The body speaks its own language long before it is close enough for facial expressions or movements of the fingers to be observed and interpreted. You have only to think of the impressions you get from a man on a bicycle perhaps fifty yards away, from a girl in a passing train, from a new teacher at the far end of a school hall. The way a person walks, sits or stands creates a strong general impression even from a distance. The tilt to the head, the angle of the shoulders, the way the elbows are held in or out, or the line of the knees when walking: all these speak a language of their own. The signals the body sends out can cover long as well as short distances and have come to have names of their own, like

Typical movement exercises of actors

'body-image' and 'non-verbal communication'.

An actor's use of his body does not stop with the kind of long-range signalling that we have been thinking of so far. It also embraces much smaller actions, like twiddling with the fingers or toes, raising eyebrows, squinting with the eyelids, smirking or pouting with the lips. These smaller, self-contained actions fall into the category of gesture rather than movement. We might define the two as follows: **movement** on the stage describes actions that involve the whole or a major

Members of the Ballet Rambert at work in one of their regular
movement classes

part of the body perhaps involving the actor in travel; **gesture** describes actions that are restricted to a specific part of the body and do not involve the actor in travel.

Few people in real life spend much time consciously organizing their movement or gesture. They rely on their natural patterns and use them, most of the time anyway, without special thought. When an actor is on the stage he is rather like a fish in a bowl or a specimen under a microscope. He is constantly being observed by the audience who will try to make sense of everything that he does. The moral is clear: every movement and gesture that an actor makes must mean something to him and should mean the same thing to an audience, although there is no guarantee that this automatically follows. Every movement and gesture of a good actor is made with style, economy of action and sensitivity.

It is when voice, speech, movement and gesture are put together skilfully by the actor, that he can be said to be acting—that is, making the play come alive by walking and talking his way through the writer's script. Just one or two examples will show how an actor's individual interpretation of a part can be put into telling action by the different ways he may choose to use the basic elements mentioned above. Take, for example, the following line:

'I tell you I'm not frightened.'

Working only on the vocal interpretation to begin with, here are only some of the possibilities. (You will probably appreciate the significance of these variations more quickly and fully if you try them out loud for yourself.) The actor may:

(a) shout	(b) whisper
(c) stammer	(d) rush the line
(e) draw it out	(f) pitch it very high

(*g*) pitch it very low

He may stress one word much more than the rest:

(*a*) 'I tell you I'm not frightened.'
(*b*) 'I **tell you** I'm not frightened.'
(*c*) 'I tell you **I'm** not frightened.'
(*d*) 'I tell you I'm **not** frightened.'
(*e*) 'I tell you I'm not **frightened**.'

He may use long pauses between words and phrases:

(*a*) 'I tell you . . . I'm not frightened.'
(*b*) 'I . . . tell you . . . I'm not . . . frightened.'
(*c*) 'I tell you I'm . . . not frightened.'
(*d*) 'I tell you I'm not . . . frightened.'

The actor can put the variations together in any way he likes and each combination will mean something different. The meaning will be further changed when the words are heard in their full context of dramatic action: movement and gesture. The following examples may precede, accompany or follow the words the actor says. In each case the meaning will be changed, marginally or radically. The actor may:

(*a*) Move from one foot to the other on the spot.
(*b*) Travel about quickly.
(*c*) Stroll about.
(*d*) Look at the people he is talking to.
(*e*) Look at his feet.
(*f*) Look over his shoulder.
(*g*) Slowly light a cigarette.
(*h*) Stub out a freshly lit cigarette.
(*i*) Spill matches on to the floor.
(*j*) Stub out a cigarette-end many times.
(*k*) Sprawl over an armchair.
(*l*) Stand on a stool.

(*m*) Lie on the floor.

(*n*) Lean against a table.

The variations are endless and they enable an actor to make the play walk and talk, to bring it to life through dramatic **characterization**. The ingredients that go to the creation of a character are:

1. What the character says when he is alone:
   (*a*) to himself
   (*b*) to the audience
2. What he says to the other characters:
   (*a*) individually
   (*b*) in groups
   either (*i*) about themselves
   or   (*ii*) about others
3. How he responds to other characters:
   (*a*) individually
   (*b*) in groups
4. What he does compared with what he says:
   (*a*) immediately
   (*b*) during the course of the play
5. What the other characters:
   (*a*) say to him
   (*b*) say about him
   (*c*) do to him
   (*d*) do about him

However, the creation of a stage character, be he hero, villain or comic, does not stop with the factors considered so far. There are two more: **make-up** and **costume**. Some actors feel that make-up and costume merely help them to *present* a character they have already created. Others feel that make-up and costume actively contribute to the creation of the character. My own view is that there is a two-way movement between an actor and his make-up and costume. The character created by the actor will suggest the kind of clothes and make-up needed. The clothes and make-up themselves will suggest changes once they are actually in action with other characters in the play.

Let us consider make-up first. Make-up is a personal matter, personal to the actor, to the character he is playing and the thoughts and feelings he has about that character. It follows that the actor himself is the best person to undertake it. It is then under his personal control at all times and nothing can replace personal experiment and practice.

The two main kinds of stage make-up are 'straight' and 'character'. A **straight** make-up is used to compensate for:

(*a*) Any make-up worn by the rest of the cast, so that no actor appears strange by comparison.

(*b*) The colour and intensity of the stage-lighting. Bright lights tend to wash out features, leaving a blank, featureless face.

(*c*) The distance of the audience. An average approach is usually taken by actors so that neither front nor back rows are unfairly treated. What might appear excellent, for example, from a back seat would probably look overdone and frightful from the front.

Actresses often wear straight day, street or evening make-up, or none at all. It all depends upon what they should *appear* to be wearing, and if this is little, then their normal make-up may be satisfactory. Generally speaking, actors should not appear to be wearing make-up at all. With the right colour and texture to their skin, there is no reason why they should not go without.

A **character** make-up is used to change the features. The

shape, colour and texture of the face and other parts of the body can be apparently transformed, but only within reasonable limits. A very fat face can be made to appear less fat, but ludicrous results would be obtained by any attempts to make it appear very thin.

The easiest form of make-up for the stage comes in sticks of greasepaint, although some actors prefer to use cakes or tubes. The colours of the make-up are identified by number or name. What is called a **foundation** is the usual remedy for the bleaching effect of strong stage lighting. The foundation is generally a combination of greasepaint colours 5 and 9.

The features of the face are given their basic shape by the use of light and shade. Light areas stand out and dark areas retreat. Light and shade also contribute to the suggestion of dramatic character in the features. The shading is most often created by white, black, grey, light and dark brown. These are only the main colours, and others are used where appropriate.

The use of other colours is generally reserved to suggest race, age and character when they are different from those of the actor playing the part. Not only the colour, but also the apparent texture of the skin is changed.

Lining adds subtle, finishing touches. It gives a bonus to the actor himself, the rest of the cast and those in the audience close enough to be able to appreciate it. Lining should always be delicately applied, otherwise the actor's face will appear to be covered with tram-lines. There are two main points to note about lining: generally, upward curving lines suggest vitality and downward lines depression, and, as might be expected, horizontal lines suggest placidity and neutrality.

The eyes and the mouth are the liveliest and most expressive parts of the face and most actors take particular care when making them up. Startlingly dramatic changes can also be made to the colour and dressing of the hair and many dyes, powders, rinses, hairpieces and wigs are used by actors and actresses.

The main steps in the application of make-up are as follows:

1. Preparation—cleaning the skin.
2. Foundation—basic colouring for race, age and character.
3. Light and shade.
4. Further colouring—character.
5. Lining—details to eyes, lips, ears, wrinkles, etc.
6. Powdering—to set the greasepaint.
7. Hair, eyebrows, eyelids—attention to final detail.

An actor's basic range of make-up would include standard sticks, liners, liquid body make-up, blending/setting powder, hair powder, crepe hair, false eyelashes, eyebrow pencils, fixative and remover for crepe hair, modelling putty, tooth enamel, blood, skin astringent or cleanser.

Turning now to costume, there are three main considerations. First, the costume should build up the actor himself as well as support the character. It is important for an actor to feel good in his stage clothes. He will then feel at ease and be more likely to give a good performance.

Second, the costume should permit all necessary stage action and encourage anything that helps the character. An actress is likely to feel impressive in a heavily embroidered, velvet cloak. If she were required to make a sweeping exit the cloak would help her, whereas this would not be so with a tight skirt.

Third, the costume should make its own statement in the overall design of the scene. On a stage where the main colour is grey, the introduction of a character dressed in scarlet will make a dramatic impact. A similar effect will be achieved from a costume in black in the midst of a scene of pale blues and pinks.

Colour in a stage costume influences the audience's response to the character wearing it and the question of our response to colour is dealt with more fully in the section on lighting below.

Line and silhouette in costume suggest a sense and feeling of period and function. Period costumes in particular are most frequently recognized by their silhouettes. In general, vertical lines in the stage clothes will suggest added height and horizontal lines added width.

The kind of material chosen for the costume will affect the way it hangs when worn. For example, the sweep of a heavy cloak cannot be achieved by the use of ordinary, light taffeta.

Let us now look at the contribution made by scenery, properties, lighting and effects. By tradition, scenery and properties go together and so do lighting and effects. In fact, their contributions are seldom appreciated separately and there is a phrase that covers the whole of the visual side of the setting: **mise-en-scène**. For clarity's sake we shall look at them under the two main sections of scenery and properties and lighting and effects, in that order.

Scenery is at one and the same time functional and decorative. A properly designed and dressed setting gives the cast a launching pad from which they can take off, and it can be sparse or lavish according to taste and budget. The three main categories into which scenery and properties fall are functional, supportive and decorative.

The **functional** are the objects physically required by the play, and essential for the action and the cast. For example, if the hero is dying in bed, the stage must show a bed, or the symbol of a bed, against a suitable background.

The **supportive** things are not essential to the action, but make it more believable to the audience and easier for the actors. These might include the chairs, bedclothes and the domestic and medical items that usually surround a sick-bed.

The **decorative** things are not essential to the action and their absence would not be noticed by the audience. Although they will help the actor in his job, they are more usually aimed at the audience to add richness and visual depth to the production. Into this section would come the decoration of the rest of the room in which the hero is dying.

Having sorted out the three main categories, it is now time to look at their style, and this is achieved by selection and rejection. After all, you can choose almost anything to put on to a stage, and what you choose will create the style. The major choices in scenery and properties lie in the following areas:

(*a*) Should the setting be **representational**? The aim of this style is to create an illusion of reality. This can be done by mixing real objects with stage representations used as substitutes when the real thing would pose serious problems on the stage—for example, flowers, trees and blood.

(*b*) Should the setting be **abstract**? The aim of this style is to use one object to suggest either more similar objects or other, different objects. For example, a throne can suggest a castle and a bed a bedroom; one military flag can suggest many flags and therefore an army; or an ordinary chair can be used as if it were a boat, a car or a ladder.

(*c*) What **physical** form should the setting take? Here there are more choices still. It can be two-dimensional, three-dimensional or projected light images on a plain background. It can be made up of a *permanent* neutral set that can represent anything throughout the play, or a *composite* set with special areas and objects that are all used at one time or another but always as the same thing. The setting can also be semi-permanent or made up of totally different units for each separate scene in the play. As a result of cinema and television, audiences are now used to swift changes of scene. The move is towards simplification and flexibility.

Settings are usually made of a combination of canvas and wood flats, with or without stage drapes, and items like rope, foam rubber, wire netting, metal foil, plastic tubes and sections, and cork, leather, hessian, straw and polystyrene.

The range of **properties** is vast. It has to be since the term covers all those articles and furnishings required by the play except the main scenic setting and costumes. There are four main types:

(*a*) **Practical:** those actually handled and used for what they are.

(*b*) **Non-practical:** additional dressing for the scene and not actually handled or used. For example, a hat stand in an entrance foyer may carry umbrellas and hats. If not used in the action the umbrellas need not open and the hats need not fit. But if they are actually used by the characters, they must work properly and be appropriate for the actors concerned.

(*c*) **Stage properties:** those on stage throughout the action of a scene and used by a number of the cast. Teapots, telephones, cushions and chairs come into this category.

(*d*) **Personal or hand properties:** those used only by specific characters, such as combs, guns, cigarette lighters, frequently kept by the actor concerned.

The collection of properties for a production can be a nightmare for the people involved. The following list gives only a few of the things that are often used: food and drinks, both hot and cold; flowers and plants; cigarettes and matches; chairs, tables and cutlery, weapons, ornaments, clocks and telephones; money, magazines, documents and letters; logs, coal and fireplaces; hallstands, tallboys and sideboards; pictures, posters and mirrors.

Neither scenery nor properties are very effective if they cannot be seen properly by the audience, and this is the point where stage lighting enters the scene, although lighting has many other uses as well. In fact, lighting is probably the most effective single device in use on the stage today. Lighting can create mood and atmosphere to such an extent that a dull room can be made to appear a place of delight and a luxuriously furbished castle a dismal tomb.

There are two main kinds of lighting equipment for the stage. They are **floods and battens**, to provide illumination evenly from a fixed position, and **spots**, to provide concentrated light upon a given area.

Lighting must be properly controlled if it is to do its job efficiently and there are three important aspects to consider: **direction, colour** and **intensity**.

Light is directed where it is wanted by simply pointing a spot at the appropriate place. Spots used without floods would give too patchy lighting, but with the right general level of illumination they create those brighter areas of light that draw the audience's attention to the important parts of the scene.

Colour is controlled by the use of filters placed in front of the spot or flood. The art and science of mixing the colours is quite complicated but in brief, when coloured light falls on a coloured object, the rule is: *like* enhances and *unlike* destroys. For example, a blue cloak under a blue light will look bluer and brighter but under a red light will look very dark, possibly even black.

There is no rule-of-thumb about the use of colour in stage lighting since everyone's response to colour is different. In

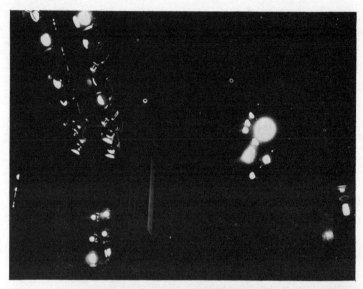

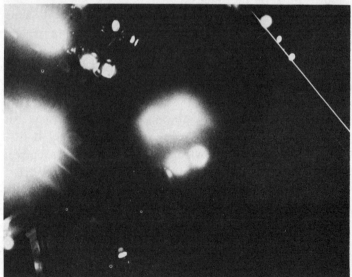

An actor's-eye-view of stage lighting

general terms, both on stage and in real life, the following
seems to apply. See if you agree.

Warm colours tend to advance—cold colours to recede.
Reds and oranges are warm and strong.
Yellow is gay and cheerful.
Blues and greens are cold and restful.
Purple and magenta are powerful and regal.
White stimulates, black depresses, grey neutralizes.

The intensity of light is controlled by the use of **dimmers**.
They enable the brightness of a light to be smoothly varied
from black-out to full brilliance. In principle they are no
different from the dimming switches used in many homes, but
they deal with the heavier electrical current that stage lighting
so often requires. This ability to vary the intensity of light
sources makes it possible to obtain the balance of lighting and
colour wanted on the stage.

Lighting is being used more and more to create a growing
range of scenic and special stage effects, which are usually
projected on to the plastered back wall of the stage area (the
cyclorama) or a plain back-cloth. Special projection lanterns
are used to throw the images, which are of two kinds:
representational and **abstract**.

Among the many representational effects are fleecy and
storm clouds, rain, snow, running water, smoke and fire.
Abstract images are even wider in their range: for example,
kaleidoscopes, spirals, catherine wheels, magic eyes, spectrum
waves and scintillating flowers. There are other special effects
using water, oils and spirits or polaroid materials and these,
with all the others, can be combined with tapes, music and the
human voice so that they come and go as the sound comes
and goes. They are also used in the many sound-and-light
shows associated with pop music and discos.

Stage effects are not all as complicated or expensive as those mentioned in the previous paragraph. Many can be created by simple, home-made machines. Most of these involve the use of sound effects and even here technology has moved in, so that many of the previously hand-operated effects are now being produced on tape. The best known are described below.

Wind machines can be made by making a slatted barrel, attaching it to an axle through its centre and covering it with a heavy canvas that can be pulled tight by hand. As the drum revolves against the canvas, a realistic wind sound is produced.

Rain machines are similar in construction, except that the canvas should be permanently attached to the drum and completely sealed off, except for a small hole to accept dried peas or their equivalent. As the drum revolves the peas create a convincing sound. There are even simpler ways, such as shaking a snare drum, dropping peas on to a tin lid or rice on to a tin tray.

Thunder machines are very simple and consist of a sheet of thin steel (3–4 feet wide and 7–15 feet long) with battens along the top and bottom edges and then freely hung. They are shaken vigorously or gently depending upon the desired effect. They may be supported by the sound of bass drums.

Crash machines can be produced by collecting pieces of ordinary glass and tin cans into one container and then pouring them—quickly or slowly as needed—into another.

Snow and rain machines are sometimes used, if the cast can be persuaded to suffer the effects of falling water or masses of confetti. The methods are fairly straightforward. For rain, a pipe with small holes in it is suspended above the stage, connected by a hose to the mains tap and turned on when needed; for snow, a cradle up to 7 or 8 feet long and cut with small slits evenly all over is suspended over the stage area. When it is shaken the confetti-snow will fall.

We have now seen how an actor and an audience grow into a subtle and complex blending of many factors: an audience willing to pretend; voice, speech, movement and gesture; make-up and costume; scenery, properties, lighting and effects. Now on to the people who work with them all, from first idea to First Night.

4 THE PEOPLE AND THEIR JOBS

THE ACTOR'S CONTRIBUTIONS IN terms of voice, speech, movement, gesture, costume and make-up have already been discussed. They are all the external aspects of his performance. The internal ones, namely his thoughts and feelings, are just as important.

An actor must be able to see and hear, clearly and with insight, how people behave and relate. He must also be able to make sense of what he sees and hears and to draw conclusions from it, conclusions that will help him remember and recreate mannerisms when he is building up a character. He must have an interest in and sympathy for people generally, because that is what his job is all about. He also needs a lively imagination, otherwise he would need to experience himself all the things he intends to share with an audience. This is not only impossible, it is also undesirable. (Think what it would mean with regard to characters like Macbeth, Othello and Hamlet.) But above all perhaps, an actor needs sensitivity and concentration so that he can work *with* the rest of the cast, and *on* the audience, perceiving and responding to what is happening to them.

Once again, we are considering what goes on during a performance, the end-product of it all. Let us now go back to square one and look at how it all started in a writer's head.

When a writer begins a play, he may have no idea where his play is going, but he does know that he cannot expect actors to get more out of his script than he puts into it. He must therefore make sure that when his script is finished it contains all the information they need to bring it to life. The more a writer wants his script to come to life in a particular way, the more must he fill it with accurate signposts. There are three main ways in which he can do this. The first is through the *dialogue*, or the actual words the actors will speak and the second through the *action*, the actual things the actors will do, stemming straight from the dialogue. The third is through *stage directions*, notes about the dialogue and action that will show even more clearly how the actors are to perform.

Most writers pay the greatest attention to the first of these, since good dialogue presents much more than just the words. It gives us an idea of the character and consequently how the actor should speak the lines, and it often tells what action should go before, with or after the lines.

On occasions the writer will specify the action separately because it will give a special meaning to the lines, and it is that meaning, and that meaning only, that the writer wishes to give to the audience.

Most good playwrights concentrate upon dialogue and action, since these are the strongest ways to move the actors and the audience. Another approach is through the instructions and directions that some playwrights, such as George Bernard Shaw, provide in detail. They may take the form of notes about clothes, character descriptions, a history of what happened before the play started, the story of what happens after it is over and, indeed, all kinds of personal statements intended to help a deeper and better understanding of the play. It is a matter of opinion whether such a playwright is being extra considerate to cast and audience, or merely trying to make up for deficiencies in his talent.

This extract from *Macbeth* by William Shakespeare shows how the dialogue itself can contain all the necessary information about the character's internal and external actions.

> Is this a dagger which I see before me,
> The handle toward my hand? Come, let me clutch thee—
> I have thee not and yet I see thee still!
> Art thou not, fatal vision, sensible
> To feeling as to sight? Or art thou but
> A dagger of the mind, a false creation,
> Proceeding from the heat-oppressèd brain?
> I see thee yet, in form as palpable
> As this which now I draw.
> Thou marshall'st me the way that I was going,
> And such an instrument I was to use.
> Mine eyes are made the fools o'the other senses,
> Or else worth all the rest. I see thee still;
> And, on thy blade and dudgeon, gouts of blood,
> Which was not so before. There's no such thing.
> It is the bloody business which informs
> Thus to mine eyes.

The next extract, from *Waiting For Godot* by Samuel Beckett, shows how specified actions bring to the text a set of meanings that would be totally absent without them. You will see that in *Macbeth* it was right for the character to speak about what he was doing. Here it is not.

VLADIMIR: Sometimes I feel it coming all the same. Then I go all queer. (*He takes off his hat, peers inside it, feels about inside it, shakes it, puts it on again.*) How shall I say? Relieved and at the same time . . . (*he searches for a word*) . . . appalled. (*With emphasis*) AP-PALLED. (*He takes off his hat again, peers inside it.*) Funny. (*He knocks on the crown as if to dislodge a foreign body, peers into it again, puts it on again.*) Nothing to be done.
   Estragon with a supreme effort succeeds in pulling off his boot.

He looks inside it, feels about inside it, turns it upside down, shakes it, looks on the ground to see if anything has fallen out, finds nothing, feels inside it again, staring sightlessly before him. Well?

ESTRAGON: Nothing.

Whatever approach the writer has taken, the result will appear as a scripted play and the next step on its journey towards production will be for a director to read it, like it and decide to bring it to life. The fact that it might be a good script at this stage does not mean that the play in production will automatically succeed. Before this comes about, the director must have been able to interpret the writer's intention and to help the cast to do the same, drawing together all the other people and elements in the production so that they contribute towards this interpretation. Above all, he must be able to share it with an audience. How does a director set about this?

His first task is to read the script—again, again and again. This enables him to explore the text until he discovers the **theme**. Every play has a theme. Every play is about something and the theme is that something. A writer may pursue his theme through a combination of characters, incidents, settings and story lines. During this first stage the director will absorb himself in the script until the author's meaning and method become crystal clear. It will then be easier for him to make sure that everything in the production bears on the central idea. In this way he can prevent irrelevant ideas, no matter how brilliant, from creeping into the play to the confusion of the audience.

His second task is to cast the play and this is usually done through brief performances from actors in what are called **auditions**. Most directors have their favourite methods, such as prepared or impromptu readings or performances of brief extracts, but their common aim is to discover those actors most likely to understand what the director has already imagined from the text. Some directors look for an almost finished product during audition and others look for a promise of imagination and creativity in spite of a hesitant performance at an audition.

The director's third task comes when the cast is assembled and ready to work. It is then his job to help them get into the body of the script for themselves. Actors need this to gain a wider vision than their own, which naturally focuses mainly on scenes which concern them. They need help to explore the text from someone who can see them at work from the outside, just as the audience will.

The director has to be a reservoir of enthusiasm, sympathy and energy. He must always be interested in the individuals who make up the cast as well as the cast as a whole. He must see that the cast grows together and at the same rate. He needs to be tolerant but not indulgent, kind but not sloppy, and compassionate but not soft. He is the ears and eyes of the audience and the guardian of the playwright. The cast will expect him to keep them together as they set about interpreting the author's meaning, skilfully blending speech and setting, voice and costume, gesture and lighting, until the whole is brought to life. To do this, a director needs imagination, sensitivity, concentration and patience. He needs an instinct for the dramatic, a feeling for ritual, a flair for magic, an ear for music and an eye for the pictorial. In brief, his job is just about impossible!

With the cast assembled and ready to work, the director may approach his rehearsal schedule in a number of ways. He may hold readings, conduct discussions, direct improvisations around scenes, characters or incidents from the play, or begin straight away on the practical work on the script. His approach will depend on the time he is given for rehearsal. An approach which gives the cast plenty of time for their personal growth would be useless in fortnightly rep, and a swift attack from all sides, giving quick but perhaps not very good results is not sensible for a cast that has six weeks to prepare a short play.

Within the overall timing set for the rehearsal period, the director has a number of choices.

He could start at the beginning of the play and work straight through to the end. This is a simple procedure and likely to get simple results, such as a satisfactory Act 1, adequate Act 2 but poor Act 3. This often happens because, unless great care is taken to make sure that rehearsal time is equally spread, the first parts may be repeated more often than the others, and too much time is spent getting the first parts right.

A different way is for crucial narrative scenes (keys to the story line of the play) to be selected and dealt with in depth, and another is for scenes involving turning points in the play or certain characters to be selected and dealt with in depth. With these two methods rehearsals then work outwards from the scenes selected. Alternatively, characters may be placed in special groupings to build up acting relationships and subsequent rehearsals may follow any of the methods mentioned above.

Scenes that are typical of the play's rhythm, language and style may be selected and worked on in depth with real rigour, concentration and discipline, until they are mastered. Rehearsals may then follow any of the methods outlined above.

There is another choice available to the director which still has some followers. Here the director works it all out in his head (or on paper and with models) and then gets the cast to bring to life his private dream as if they were a set of puppets. Such a rigid approach has little to recommend it. All that can be said is that it is likely to run to schedule and be satisfying for the director.

During the rehearsal period the director will also be giving his attention to those aspects of the production usually linked together under the heading of **stage management**. Here he may have the services of skilled specialists, although the smaller the company the more he and the cast will have to double up on many jobs. Although these jobs will now be described as if they were entirely separate, in practice they are not. The reasons for this are the shortage of manpower mentioned above and the fact that everyone is working towards a unified production, not the collection of isolated parts. The organization and blending of the various parts is one of the director's most difficult tasks, especially since many of his colleagues may be gifted not only with professional skills but also with explosive temperaments to match.

When the time comes for the director to turn to the stage management aspects (and this will vary from individual to individual) he will first consult the people responsible for scenic, costume and lighting design. All of them will have studied the script and some may have attended early re-hearsals. There may be separate designers for the three areas or there may be only one. In turn, they may have separate teams of carpenters, painters, sempstresses and electricians to undertake the detailed work. If the production is a large one and there is no shortage of money or manpower, the working team might be as follows.

The **Director**, who has overall responsibility for the crea-tive, interpretative and artistic aspects of the production. He should not be confused with the Producer, who is concerned with hiring and firing, and the business management to do with the production and the theatre.

The **Senior Stage Manager**, who has overall responsibility for the smooth running of the stage and its resources at all times.

The **Stage Manager**, who has overall responsibility for the general instructions of the Director and the Designer for setting, lighting, properties, costume, music and sound.

The **Designers**, who are responsible to the Director for creating blue-prints (sketches, scale-drawings or models) that can be easily interpreted and made.

The **carpenters and painters**, who are responsible to the Stage Manager for the making and finishing of all scenery.

A stage carpenter at work on a flat

The **electricians**, who are responsible to the Stage Manager for the installation and operation of all lighting equipment and electrically operated sound effects.

The **Property Master**, who is responsible to the Stage Manager for the provision (and often creation), correct placing and storing (on and off stage) of all articles used in the production except major scenery and lighting. He may have several assistants.

The **Wardrobe Mistress**, who is responsible to the Stage Manager for the provision (and often creation), storage and good repair of all costumes. She may also have assistants.

The **stage crew**, who are responsible to the Stage Manager for the correct arranging and changing of all scenic items. Some of this crew may also be responsible for any manual effects.

The **Prompter**, who is responsible to the Stage Manager during rehearsals, helping the cast to eliminate errors of recall, and during performances, acting as a safety net in case an actor should 'dry' or give a wrong cue. The prompter must know both play and players better than anyone else and has an important but thankless task.

Many of these people are known by the initials of their job. For example, SM is the Stage Manager. One of the most famous sets of initials is ASM, meaning Assistant Stage Manager. Often this title means that the company cannot afford to employ any of the people mentioned in the list above who are responsible to the Stage Manager. Under such circumstances the ASM does the lot, including sweeping the stage and making the tea!

Not all companies are large enough to afford understudies for all, or even most of the parts. With a complicated production and a number of large parts, understudy or doubling up arrangements must be made, or there should be on call suit-

A lighting crew setting up before a show
The stage-lighting control panel (or console) at the Royal Court Theatre

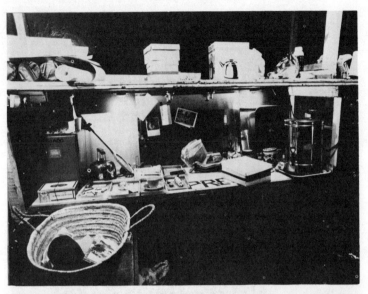

Properties ready for use during a performance of *Life Class*
The stage crew preparing for a performance of *Life Class*

A typical back-stage dressing-room to be shared by two or three actors

able stand-ins who can memorize very quickly. Actors are not immune from accidents or sickness and there is the tradition that the 'show must go on'. Understudies substitute under these circumstances. Being an understudy can provide useful training but, because of its very nature, it can never be very fulfilling.

Much of the music in the theatre today is provided from disc or tape and is generally known as 'incidental' music, mainly because it is associated with the performance only, and in the exact meaning of the word, incidentally. If a stage production needs live musicians on-stage, back-stage or in the orchestra pit, there will usually be a Musical Director who will work closely with both the Stage Manager and the Director.

So far, this chapter has been concerned with the people who work under the overall direction of the Director. There are also many other people who are just as necessary to the smooth running of the theatre and therefore to the production. They are known as the 'front-of-the-house staff' (usually by the initials FOH) and are responsible to the theatre management. This group of people looks after the needs of the audience and serves its area, generally referred to as the auditorium. The work covers a vast range of activities including the running of the box-office and the sale of tickets, programmes, sweets and chocolates, the running of the bars, showing theatregoers to their seats; and, not to be forgotten, cleaning.

From the first idea in a writer's head to a first performance on stage is, as we have seen, a complicated business, employing many people with vastly differing skills. Central to the whole process is the writer's script, providing the point of departure, the route and destination in a play that comes alive on the stage.

Theatre cleaners taking a well-deserved break
The box-office at the Royal Court Theatre

5 PLAYS AND PERFORMANCES

AS WE HAVE ALREADY SEEN, the earliest plays did not have scripts. There were no writers to make them since there was no writing. As civilization changed, reading and writing became more important and plays moved from their first focus on the Sun, the Moon and the Universe 'out there'; to gods in the form of huge and dangerous animals; to gods in the form of huge and dangerous humans; to humans in the form of gods, kings and leaders; and finally, today, to humans in the form of humans, many plays being about ordinary people in ordinary situations.

Nowadays a playwright has many sources for an idea for a play. It may come from myth, legend, a novel, another play or it may be a quite original idea, difficult though it is to dream up something new. Some playwrights spend a lot of time just sitting thinking, waiting for inspiration to come to them; others carry on normal life waiting for an interesting event, watching and listening to their friends, acquaintances and people at large, just in case something useful may turn up; and others spend weeks, even months, in research, hoping to find facts and features that will add up to the making of a play.

Some playwrights write slowly and methodically, others very fast and off the top of their heads. Some plan their play first and others just let it grow, having no idea how it will end

or how many characters might enter the scene. But whichever
way the playwright tackles his writing, the end-product today
is always a **script**. We have seen how complicated the process
of putting on a play can be, yet the ingredients for all those
processes must be contained in the script. This is not a simple
job at the best of times and is often difficult for new writers
who have little experience of what really goes on in the theatre.
Here are the views of two playwrights about how they set
about their job. The first is a brief reminder from the preface
to Ann Jellicoe's *Sport of My Mad Mother*: it 'was not written
intellectually according to a prearranged plan. It was shaped
bit by bit until the bits felt right in relation to each other and
to the whole . . .'

The second comes from an old hand in the theatre, William
Saroyan, and it describes some of his feelings about working
on a play with the company that was going to perform it.
Here is what he says in the preface to *Sam the Highest Jumper
of Them All*: 'From Paris in February of 1960 I wrote to Joan
Littlewood to say that I had enjoyed seeing Brendan Behan's
play *The Hostage* in London. The manager of the Theatre
Royal, Gerald Raffles, replied and invited me to direct one of
my own plays at the Theatre Royal. I sent him three published
plays and two ideas I had for new plays. He chose one of the
three, *Jim Dandy*, but a few days later he wondered if I might
be able to make a play in the theatre out of one of the ideas.
I said I could, although the procedure would make great demands on the players. On 16 March I arrived in London and
went to work, meeting players and writing the play. A rough
draft was finished in nine or ten days. Two benefit performances were given in April, and on the 6 April the play
opened to the press and the general public. The house was
packed and the response of the audience gave me the impression that they liked it. The reviews, however, informed me

that the play was meaningless and amateurish.'

Agreement about what makes a good play has eluded generations of writers, audiences and critics. In very general terms only, a good play usually has the following qualities:

It gives enrichment, insight and joy.

It creates intense experiences, stimulates the imagination and provokes responses.

It does not make dogmatic statements, but poses questions about human behaviour; sadness and happiness; joy and despair; the search for security; and the fear of death.

It has a marked rhythm and style all of its own.

Its language invites speaking. It asks, if not demands, to be said out loud.

It can be encountered many times without any lessening of interest. Each time it offers deeper and broader interpretations.

It celebrates the joys and fears of being human.

It can be approached at many levels, being deep and profound without being obscure, and speaking directly to everyone in a language they can understand, yet not sinking into clichés or triviality.

It carries the ring of truth of one man's vision of what life and death, love and hate can do to us. It tells of those parts of ourselves that we often try to hide, not only from each other but also from ourselves.

In brief, a good play sets out to make us more aware of ourselves, other people and the world around us. This does not mean that it must be sombre, high-toned and moralizing. The process can be painless and even good fun, but this, too, is a matter of personal taste and therefore a subject for debate. For example, *Waiting for Godot* by Samuel Beckett appealed to audiences in Paris as enjoyable *entertainment* (the word coming from the Latin for 'to grip' or 'to hold') while most audiences in London found it intellectual, arty and heavy going.

Many people say they go to the theatre to be entertained, meaning they want to be helped to relax or to be taken out of themselves. One can be taken out of oneself in order to understand oneself more clearly or in order to forget oneself and escape from everyday responsibilities. There are plays that cater for both tastes. There are also plays that take us more deeply into ourselves. Broadly speaking, tragedy looks inward to the nature of people and comedy stands back and looks at how people get on with one another. Both set out to help us control and organize our lives, tragedy helping make sense of ourselves and comedy helping us make sense of other people. But both are intended to help us get more out of life, other people and, therefore, ourselves.

Not long ago, plays were divided into three clear categories: **tragedy**, **comedy** and **melodrama**. Tragedies had unhappy endings, comedies happy ones and melodramas were plays with music. In Shakespeare's day, the middle ground between tragedy and comedy was called, as you might expect, **tragicomedy**. Today, the edges are blurred and **drama** covers the many categories in the middle ground.

We have recently come to understand, and to include in our plays, the idea that a person without high social or political status does not have to be little inside. Perhaps two of the most well-known attempts are *Death of a Salesman* by Arthur Miller and *A Streetcar Named Desire* by Tennessee Williams. There is little doubt that the leading figures in both are tragic, although the action is domestic.

As suggested earlier, it is the social element that makes a play a comedy, not its ability to make us laugh. In fact, some comedies make us laugh and some do not. Some make us laugh at ourselves and some at other people. Although this is not the place to discuss the nature and purpose of laughter, it is true to say that we often laugh out of relief, either as a release of tension or as simple delight that we were not involved in the event.

Satire and **farce** are two kinds of comedy that set out to make us laugh—the first at ourselves (satire always carries a sting in its tail) and the second at other people. Satire is generally intellectual, and farce knock-about physical. They both exaggerate to gain their effects but whereas serious ideas about people and things lie behind the laughter of satire, farce is usually content to operate at the level of custard pies and clergymen in their underclothes.

The types of play considered so far may all use different styles of construction and different kinds of language. The following categories are only the main ones, but they are not rigid and one play may borrow from several categories.

The **Theatre of Naturalism** is probably the best-known type of play today. There are many varieties in this school ranging from dramatized documentaries and the slice-of-life, to kitchen-sink dramas and drawing-room comedies, but all involve mainly ordinary situations with ordinary people and are undoubtedly popular among theatregoers. The essence of this type of play lies in two features: the actors play the parts of ordinary people behaving in a normal manner, and both audience and players pretend that they are not in a theatre. The players pretend all the time, and the audience most of the time, that neither group is aware of the other's presence.

Naturalism is often called **Realism**, but since the aim of all good plays is to expose the reality of living this is a confusing title. (For that matter, so is Naturalism, since theatre must, by its very nature be artificial. A more accurate title for the school of plays covered by this 'natural' style of acting is perhaps, **Behaviourism.**)

Into this category comes a special kind which should be mentioned, even though it is no longer fashionable. That is the *well-made play*, and it is written to a formula in which every scene, character and situation is balanced by another equal and opposite in effect. The plays are constructed so that both sides of any question or statement are dealt with equally.

Completely opposite to so-called naturalism is the **Theatre of Symbolism**. Its most important sub-division is called **Expressionism**. In these plays, actors do not play ordinary people, but instead represent their thoughts, feelings and actions by special symbols and conventions. The actors often play a less important role than the scenery, music, sound and light effects, special costume, make-up and masks, and many other stage devices that are seldom used in naturalistic plays. They also have to play the parts of abstract things such as Power, Fear, Knowledge, and while some of the plays can over-simplify their subject matter, many achieve the strength and dignity of their forerunners, the Medieval Morality Plays. Two of the best known plays of this type are *Masses and Men* (*Masse-Mensch*) by Ernst Toller, and *The Insect Play* (also known as *The Life of the Insects* and *And so ad infinitum*) by Josef and Karel Capek.

Very close to symbolism is the **Theatre of Cruelty**, which uses a mixture of styles. The name is often misused and little understood, as the plays in this style are not cruel or violent as such but stem from a set of ideas outlined and championed by Antonin Artaud. The plays create a type of theatre which has more in common with a psychedelic disco than the average stage play. They involve the use of music, song and dance; the plastic arts; dumb show, cries and moans; puppets and film; moving scenery and architecture; flashing lights and travelling sound-sources; and incantation and ritual. The style sets out to involve the audience by an assault on the senses.

Removed from this style of play is the **Theatre of Alienation** (Verfremdungseffekt) created in the main by Bertolt Brecht, who wanted to bring about a state of critical detachment in his audiences. Plays of this type set out to prevent actual involvement on the part of the audience. They use a stylized form of acting that draws attention to itself, often aided by posters, banners and placards; films, cartoons and documentary projections, or any device that will remind the audience that they are seeing a *representation of and commentary on* life, and *not* life itself.

The **Theatre of the Absurd** covers a type of play that sets out to show that life is basically pointless; that existence itself is a doubtful proposition, and that any form of human communication is impossible. In brief, we are all absurd, involved in an absurd situation. It is not the basic idea behind the plays that has made the Theatre of the Absurd a significant development, but the fact that it released writers from the straitjacket of orthodox dramatic form and normal language, enabling them to experiment freely and bring many fresh ideas into the theatre. Its main exponents live and work in France and the two best known are Samuel Beckett and Eugene Ionesco.

Whatever the style of play, *language* plays an important part one way or another. The three main categories of dramatic language are *naturalistic* (in which normal conversation is used), *poetic* (in which language is heightened for effect, the minimum number of words being used to obtain the maximum impact) and *symbolic* (in which voice and speech are used experimentally, with an emphasis upon chant, song and incantation).

These classifications of types of play and language are only

the main ones and there are many exceptions and contradic-
tions. But even so, they do not stop there, although we are
now going to move out of the area occupied by orthodox
stage plays. The first main division comes with those stage
presentations that concentrate upon the use of *music, song*
and *dance*. Generally speaking, these pieces set out to make
us feel rather than think, but they invite us to respond as does
any form of theatre from a football Cup Final to an intimate
poetic tragedy. Music and song combine to create *operas* and
musicals in which the stage spectacle and the music tend to
be much more important than the words (the libretto or any
intervening 'normal' dialogue). Music and movement combine to create *ballets*, *dance-dramas* and *mimes* (though some
important examples of these exist without music). Here again
the element of spectacle is always important, but the music
plays less of a central role than in operas.

Of less frequent occurrence now than in the earlier part of
the century are pantomime, music-hall and revue. The same
thing can be said about certain forms of plays that do not use
live actors, such as puppet shows, shadow plays and the well-
known but little seen Punch and Judy theatres. Other forms
of plays without actors are, however, gaining more interest.
Son et Lumiére performances in castles, cathedrals, discos
and pop festivals are becoming very popular. Most of them
use the natural or architectural setting of the event as a piece
of stage scenery with special lighting. Generally, the music
and dialogue are pre-recorded and played back through a
multitude of speakers. Many top-ranking actors and actresses
have taken part in these eye-catching spectacles.

Some plays have been specially written for performance
inside theatres, but still without using live actors. The following brief extract from:

```
                    . K–M
                       .
       O–B–A–F–G– .
                   .   .
                  .   .
                 .    . R–N
                 .
                 S          by Ronald Duncan
```

gives something of the idea:

No actors are required.

The stage remains bare throughout except for rostra piled to cast effective shadows.

At the beginning of the play, both the stage and the auditorium should be in *absolute* darkness (exit signs should be switched off and measures taken to prevent *any* light penetrating the theatre).

During the absolute darkness *complete* silence should be endured for as long as the audience can bear it. When they become restless, a metronome is heard (very soft to very loud).

Listening to it, the audience achieves silence again.

The metronome recedes till the audience have to strain their ears for the comfort of its sound.

It is completely silent again and still absolutely dark.

LOUDSPEAKER NO. 1

(girl's voice) Mummy, why is it so dark?

(woman's voice) I don't know, dear.

LOUDSPEAKER NO. 2

There is no light

Unless there is something for it to shine upon. (*a long pause*)

LOUDSPEAKER NO. 1

(girl's voice) Mummy, why is it so silent?

(woman's voice) I don't know, dear.

LOUDSPEAKER NO. 2

Nor can sound exist

Until there is an ear to hear it.

LOUDSPEAKER NO. 1

Mummy, I'm frightened.

LOUDSPEAKER No. 2
  So you should be, my dear.
  . . . .
  (*The sound of the metronome very soft to silent.*)
  then, then, then, then, then
  (*Instantaneous full light on stage and audience and simultaneously the sound of explosions. The light is immediately switched off except for red spots beamed on to the ceiling.*)

From plays without actors it is not a far cry to plays without theatres, and undoubtedly the largest audiences are to be found watching films in cinemas, or at home watching films and plays on television or listening to plays on the radio. These three media have brought more people into touch with drama of one kind or another than ever before. Two major factors separate these forms of drama from the theatre. The first is that audiences may vary from millions (in large numbers in large cinemas or ones and twos at home) to thousands, but they will be scattered in time and place and there is no direct contact between audience and players. The second factor is that visual aspects play no part in radio drama, and in film and television effects can be so easily and quickly made that they often show the limitations of the theatre.

Plays without theatres are not restricted to the three media mentioned above. Many actors and directors find their work more challenging when they take it into streets, beaches, pubs, clubs, cafés and even prisons. Joan Littlewood, probably best known for her work at the Theatre Royal in East London, has had plans for many years to produce theatre in inflatable tents, hoping for an atmosphere more like the Fun-Palace than the usual kind of theatre.

In *As You Like It*, Shakespeare wrote: 'All the world's a stage, and all the men and women merely players.' So now on to the world of the theatre's platform, its '*bare boards*', to see the great variety of shapes and sizes the stage has had in the past and has to offer today.

6 THEATRES AND STAGES

THE HISTORY OF THE THEATRE
is long and complex, and the history of stages—those spaces used by only the special few—is similar. Just a few examples will show something of the variety of its 'passing show'.

The Egyptians used open-air theatres with casts of thousands and mass public participation. The Chinese performed operatic rituals in small inner rooms. The Indians and Greeks used open-air temples and the Romans had their sacrificial amphitheatres. There have been stages in booths, cockpits and inn-yards; in churches and the entrances to churches; and on bare wooden boards on horse-drawn carts. The Italians invented elaborate closed boxes to show off their mastery of visual perspective. Travelling players of the past used horses and simple carts. Those of the present use huge vans and collapsible platforms to create fully equipped mobile theatres. The variety is tremendous, but the basic idea remains the same: a place for an artificial 'let's pretend' conflict between Man and Superman (and Superman can represent another man, a group of men—or women, a nation or a god).

Historically, the main difference in theatres was between the open-air and the roofed-over. Today, the main difference in stages is between the 'open' and the 'closed'. Before con-

A mannequin parade
A wrestling match

A Punch and Judy show

sidering the history of stage shapes, we will look at present-day versions of open and closed stages. They each have their merits and drawbacks, and each is defended vigorously by its supporters. Not long ago, the proscenium stage, an example of the closed version, dominated the theatre, but more open and flexible types have recently been built.

On the traditional closed stage the audience and actors are physically separated from one another; on the open stage they share the same space and often the same lighting. The open stage offers many possibilities for real contact, involvement and participation between actors and audiences. The closed stage cannot compete in this area and, instead, specializes in presenting stage pictures where magic and mystery can be created without the audience ever being able to see the machinery that creates these effects.

Some experts maintain that some plays are more suited to one type of stage than others. There is no hard and fast rule and each director must make up his own mind whether he needs an open or a closed stage for his production.

The two main ways of providing a stage area are as follows:

1. A permanent stage area built to give as much flexibility as possible within a fixed and clearly defined structure. Most professional theatres tend to be of this type.

2. A clear space in an open hall with a flat floor, equipped with movable lighting and rostrum blocks to create seating and stage areas.

The main types of open and closed stages are now described and illustrated. The following key is used for the illustrations:

A = Audience	⟶ = Sight Lines
X = Acting Areas	W = Wings
⌇⌇⌇ = Curtains	- - - - = Possible variations

Closed Stages

Proscenium. The proscenium type stage is usually raised above floor level and the audience can be seated above or below that level. The seating is often stepped in tiers (*raked*) to improve the sight lines for the audience. The proscenium stage is essentially a box with one side only open to the audience.

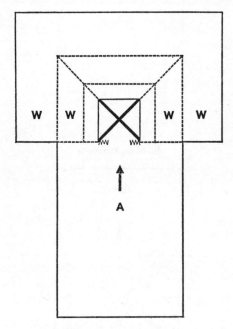

Proscenium stage (closed)

End. The end stage is a variation of the proscenium stage with the opening to the audience covering the full width of the auditorium. The stage is often level with the first row of seating. End stages can also be built in open versions (see p. 75).

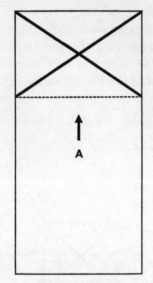

End stage (closed)

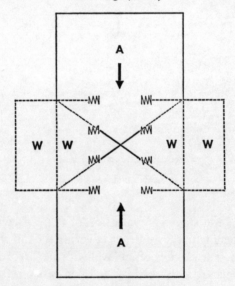

Central stage (closed)

Central. This is a very special version of the proscenium stage. It is still essentially a box but instead of the one opening there are now two and the audience sits on two sides, facing each other across the stage area. Central stages can also be built in open versions. Both end and closed central stages are found infrequently in England.

Open Stages

Arena. Arena stages can be built to be square or circular, rectangular or triangular, and the halls they are built in can be large or small. It is usual for them to be small with a small seating capacity. The aim of this is to create a sense of intimacy between actors and audience. The audience completely surrounds the acting area and actors and audiences share the same total space within the auditorium. Sometimes they share the same lighting.

End. The actors and the audience share the same total space within the auditorium. The audience does not completely surround the acting area. The actors have a background in front of which they can perform and behind which they can usually get changed.

Thrust. Thrust stages usually are raised above floor level. The audience sits on three sides, surrounding the acting area more than in the end stage. Actors and audience still share the same total space within the auditorium.

Avenue. The avenue stage is a special version of the central stage and examples of it are to be found more and more frequently. Actors and audience share the same total auditor-

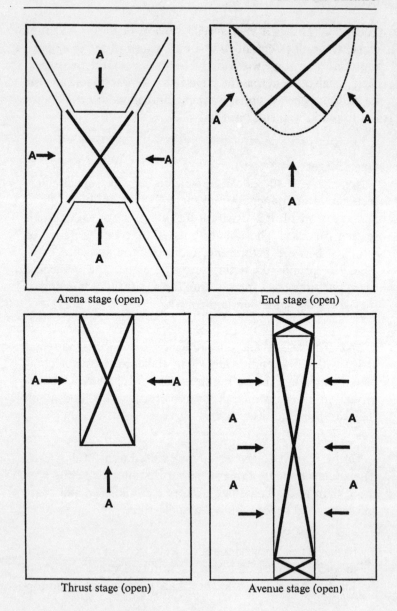

Arena stage (open)

End stage (open)

Thrust stage (open)

Avenue stage (open)

ium space and it is perhaps most effective when productions need two settings which are markedly contrasted, and a third which is for common use (perhaps representing many different places).

Space. These types of stages are quite different from all the others so far. Instead of the audience surrounding the stage, the stage surrounds the audience. The acting areas are more like isolated 'stations' and are often raised above floor level. Generally, the actors and the audience share the same total space of the auditorium, although in some special cases closed stages are used on the edges of the audience areas. Very often, swivel chairs are needed so that the audience can change the direction of its sight lines easily and at will.

Total Theatre

The simplest version of the total theatre type of production is to be seen in plays like *Rose and Crown* by J. B. Priestley and *The Man with the Flower in his Mouth* by Luigi Pirandello, where the layout and furnishings of the auditorium represent the public house and the restaurant where the action in these plays occurs. The audience are treated as 'customers' by the actors and the play is presented with complete naturalism. There is little formality until the drama of the action takes over.

In its more experimental forms the total theatre production seems to *attack* the audience with an assault on all its senses. There may be journeys from hall to hall, stage to stage and a continuing bombardment from actors, loudspeakers, lights, films, slides, television and even moving scenery. The

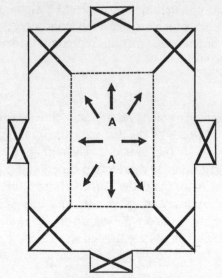

Space stage (with inner stage)

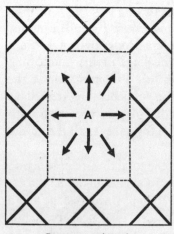

Space stage (open)

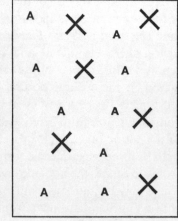

Space stage (scattered or integral)

audience may be required (without notice and with little choice) to participate, to improvise, to spectate as at a football match, to move freely about the space or to be led by members of the cast on a long trip. Presentation techniques include those of the music-hall, ballet, circus, strip-clubs, encounter groups, political rallies and even the school classroom.

The picture today would not be complete without an example of a purpose-built flexible theatre. The illustrations that follow show something of the adaptability of the Octagon Theatre, Bolton, where it is possible to move from open end, to thrust stage to theatre-in-the-round productions within the same stage/theatre space.

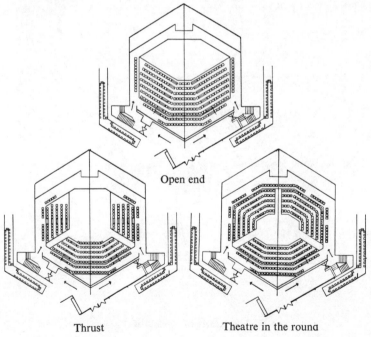

Open end

Thrust   Theatre in the round

The rest of this chapter is given over to illustrations that show the main trends and shapes from the earliest times to the present day. The story speaks for itself through the pictures.

The theatre of Epidaurus

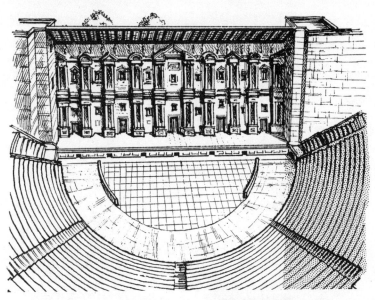

The Roman theatre of Aspendos
Commedia dell'Arte travelling theatre 'fit-up'

Harlequin—a character from the Commedia dell'Arte

A medieval pageant play

A typical theatre of Shakespeare's time

Part of the stage of the Teatro Olimpico at Vicenza, 1579

A Renaissance theatre
An open-air performance of *Le Malade Imaginaire*, before the King
and court at Versailles, 1674

The Drury Lane Theatre, 1808

An early performance of *School for Scandal*

A scene from a Georgian play

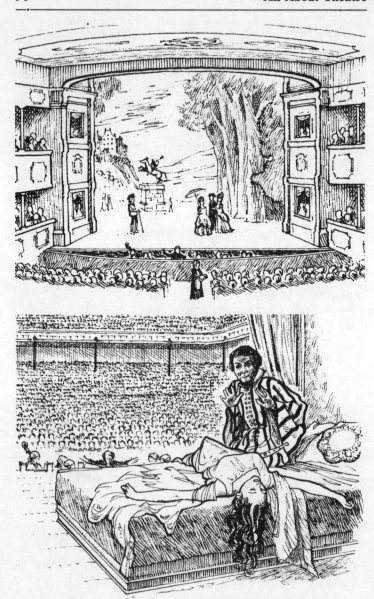

A Georgian Theatre
Othello at the Regency Theatre, Tottenham Street, London, 1817

The Cockpit Theatre, London

The Octagon Theatre, Bolton
The Mermaid Theatre, London

The Festival Theatre, Chichester

The Festival Theatre, Ontario, Canada

7 A PLAY COMES TO LIFE

IT SHOULD BE CLEAR BY NOW that there is no one way of rehearsing and producing a script, of bringing a play to life. Every good play has a life of its own .·. . and a different life for each production.

In this chapter I shall outline how one production of one script came to life at one particular time.

Life Class, written by David Storey and directed by Lindsay Anderson, was first produced at the Royal Court Theatre, London, in April 1974. The script is a personal statement by the playwright; the production is a personal interpretation by the director; and the following description is an account of my own observations and discussions with the team of *Life Class*.

In a work of art it is not generalized effort by organized groups that creates a lasting impression, but the individual contributions by different people. When it comes to making a play those concerned can only give what they personally possess . . . and those who watch can only take what they are capable of taking. It is all personal, and that is what makes works of art exciting, challenging and unique.

It follows that this chapter is probably the most important and the most difficult. Any good production is *more than the sum of its parts*. The parts themselves are difficult enough to

Two views of the exterior of the Royal Court Theatre during the run of
Life Class

describe, but the 'little bit more' (the extra factor) is even more so. With a jig-saw puzzle it is obvious when there is an extra bit, but not so in the production of a play. Everyone concerned with the production of *Life Class* stressed the importance of the *extra factor*. This was not to create a mystique. It was to help explain how the extra factor makes for magical, memorable moments of theatre—moments they are constantly trying to achieve, and that more than justify the years of training, the hard work, being out of work, the gruelling rehearsals and the demanding performances. They are the moments when theatre excels, and everyone is gripped by them. They are what theatre is all about.

The team of *Life Class* worked generally within a method involving the ideas and feelings associated with these words: *trust, intuition, empirical, spontaneous, group, sensitivity*, and *open*. For the moment, one or two phrases may help explain the company's approach:

'Chance enters the prepared mind'—and a mind not *open* can never be prepared.

'Creation by accident: art by design'—and a mind not *open* cannot recognize or manipulate a creative accident.

A quotation from *The Cocktail Party* by T. S. Eliot— it was written about people but I use it here to refer to a production:

> To approach the stranger
> Is to invite the unexpected, release a new force,
> Or let the genie out of the bottle.
> It is to start a train of events
> Beyond your control.

To work on a play is to approach a stranger, and *inviting the unexpected and releasing new forces* is exactly what rehearsals are about. Certain procedures are essential. They are: rejecting the predictable; avoiding the probable; and exploiting the possible to bring about glimpses of the perfect but impossible.

The team of *Life Class* seemed convinced that these procedures were most likely to bring about the 'little bit more' or the extra factor. It is important to realize, however, that this extra factor is not the only thing that makes a good production come to life. No inspired act of theatre can ever emerge without hard work, commitment, expertise and talent. No one concerned with *Life Class* ignored this when they stressed the importance of the extra factor. They were well aware of working with a sense of purpose . . . and to strict disciplines. There was neither haphazard sloppiness nor frenzied flailing about. They relied primarily on sheer hard work and the method based upon the words mentioned above.

Some definitions may help get across what these meant to the team.

Trust: confidence in the truth of anything; confident expectation; a resting on the integrity of another; faith; hope.

Intuition: the power of the mind by which it immediately perceives the truth of things without reasoning or analysis.

Empirical: resting upon trial or experiment; known or knowing only by experience.

Spontaneous: acting by its own impulse or natural law; produced of itself.

Group: a number of individual things related in some definite way to make them different from others; a combination of figures forming a harmonious whole.

Sensitivity: feeling readily, acutely or painfully; ready and delicate in reactions.

In the rest of this chapter I do not try to analyse or criticize

Life Class, but to highlight a few features that contributed to its final effect and helped to make it a play with a life of its own.

I chose two sections of the play (one lasting a mere moment, the other a few minutes) and asked about their beginning, growth and meaning. The first was the opening of the play. In performance, Allott's entrance was exactly as the script indicates:

The cast and set of *Life Class* in action during performance

ACT ONE

A stage.

Off-centre, stage-right, is a wooden platform, some six to eight feet square, on castors.

Beside it are two metal stands, about six feet high, each equipped with two vertical flat-plate heaters.

Scattered around the platform are several wooden 'donkeys': low rectangular stools with an upright T-shaped bat at one end. On one, folded, is a white sheet.

There are two brown hessian screens, one upstage centre, the other centre left. Upstage left is a rack with coatpegs.

ALLOTT comes in stage-left.

In his late thirties, medium build, he wears a duffle-coat, battered trilby hat, and gloves.

Blows in his hands. Thumps gloves.

Shivers.

The italics are mine. I thought the action to be ineffectual and possibly contradictory (since blowing through leather gloves does not warm one's hands). I wondered if it meant something special about Allott or if it was a stage cliché not worth thinking about. Since it was part of the opening action of the play I followed it up.

The first person to turn to was the director, Lindsay Anderson. I put my points to him more or less as described above. For a moment or two he was silent. Then he said, 'Ah, yes . . . I remember. Well, it always happened and just seemed right so I didn't think about it any more.'

I asked for his permission to approach the cast about this particular gesture. (Very important this, since any creative director is more than justified in being sensitive at an outsider peering into his head.)

I then talked to Anton Gill, the assistant to the director. After a few minutes of discussion he said, 'In any case, for the character, I have always thought the gesture to be rational, credible and not without meaning. But, more important than all that, it seemed right for the opening of the play.'

I mentioned the moment to many others concerned with the production, including members of the cast. Some thought there could be a contradiction between the gesture and its meaning but others felt it was not particularly important.

I also raised the point with more than twenty members of the audience at different times. Not one of them remembered the gesture. They could all recall that the play began with Allott appearing and being cold. One of them said: 'Well, he must have been cold mustn't he, because he went to put on the gas fires' (in fact, the heaters were electric!).

Allott, played by Alan Bates

I next approached Allott, played by Alan Bates, and put my question. He looked at me for a long time: 'I don't know . . . I don't know. Well, there is really only one answer; it says so in the script.' This cleared the way for a longer conversation in which he told me about the opening few seconds of the play. One thing led me logically to the author. It seems that during rehearsals and even early performances Alan Bates had not always got everything perfect and he also remembered David Storey placing particular stress upon the shiver referred to in the script. He was definite that the author felt the shiver to be of real importance and that if he omitted anything in the opening seconds, it was always the shiver.

This shiver was one of the first things I put to David Storey. He did not remember stressing the shiver and was mildly surprised to hear what Alan Bates had said. He did recall mentioning that he thought the opening moments of the play appeared to be over too quickly and that perhaps something might be done about it. All this supports the intuitive method of working since the author, the director and the actor were all content that the opening was then all right, but each had got there from different viewpoints and without thinking about it at length. If, for example, the author had spelled out in another way that he felt the opening to be over too soon, something quite different might have happened, and it might not have been as satisfactory. Simply by mentioning, as he said 'off the top of his head', the shiver, everyone got what they wanted. This discussion led naturally to my query about the blowing on the gloved hands. After a long silence, David Storey said: 'That blowing on the gloved hands seemed to underline the ineffectualness of Allott, the man and his life.'

So the creative cycle turns. In the end, the only thing that really matters about this opening scene is that an actor playing the part of Allott appears on a stage in flesh and blood before a living audience and does what he has to do. But in order to get to that moment, and to make sure the moment is right, many other things must occur, and all the way through there are many opportunities for what we have been calling the 'extra factor'. My inquiry into this particular moment has shown that it can come about in different ways. My purpose is not to expose inefficiency but to show that in a worthwhile act of theatre there is a collection of diversities that, one way or another, make up a uniform whole.

The second section I chose reflects some of the problems and their solutions in a more complicated piece of dramatic action. Here is the text of the scene:

MATHEWS: First time I've seen his drawing.

PHILIPS: One of the leading exponents of representational art in his youth was Mr Allott . . . You'd have to go back to Michaelangelo to find a suitable comparison . . .

      (MATHEWS stoops over pad: peers closely.)

MATHEWS: There's nothing there . . .

PHILIPS: Now, of course . . . an impresario . . . purveyor of the invisible event . . . so far ahead of his time you never see it.

MATHEWS: I've been posing there for half an hour!

PHILIPS: Longer I'd imagine.

. . . .

MATHEWS (reads): 'O we'll listen to the wireless
    And lie in bed till three;
    "Turn up the volume, lady."
    O, love is good to me.'

      (Evades PHILIPS' effort to take the pad.)

    'O he found love in valleys,
    In caves and crannies too;
    Fissures, where a lover
    Could find what lovers do.'

PHILIPS: I think, really, that belongs to me . . . is in my custody
. . . my supervision.

MATHEWS (reads): 'He called her night and morning;
  He sat beside the phone:
  What's mine is yours, she told him:
  O give a dog a bone!'

PHILIPS: I'm appealing to you, Mathews, as a member of the
staff . . . as a respected and somewhat elderly member of the
staff . . . lightweight champion of the northern counties and—
for several months previous to that—of one of the more
prominent of the southern counties as well.

MATHEWS (reads): 'He waited, how he waited;
  He waited for his love:
  She'd meant to get there early,
  But went back for her glove.'

PHILIPS: See here, Mathews . . . That's private property.

MATHEWS: Here . . . just look at this.

(Shows it to PHILIPS.)

PHILIPS (reads): 'I shall kill Foley . . . Foley is very poorly . . .
Foley is surely . . .
  the person I shall hourly . . .
  kill . . .
  whenever poor old Allott gets the chance . . .'

In performance this encounter between Philips and
Mathews was a complex piece of choreographed action.
Philips has to appear to want to get the pad from Mathews
and to confront him physically. He cannot be allowed to do
this otherwise the psychological basis of his character would
be broken; the dramatic action already created would cease;
and the direction of the play would be switched. No matter
how logical the encounter may appear to be, nor how necessary it may seem from a number of points of view, it must be
prevented, and the way of preventing it must be made credible
to the audience.

Allott and Mathews during performance

In *Life Class*, the director's method of achieving the desired effect was to exploit the character of Philips: apparently always ready to make a move but never doing so until certain it would not succeed.

After this scene within a scene, the relationships change: for example

MATHEWS: Here . . . just look at this.

(Shows it to PHILIPS.)

PHILIPS (reads): 'I shall kill Foley . . . Foley is very poorly . . . Foley is surely . . .'

From this moment on, in this scene, Mathews and Philips become, in a sense, not two separate characters, but one character within two bodies, so far as the dramatic action is concerned. The earlier minor ritual of posing and physical distancing on stage, created without loss of credibility, was only achieved after strictly disciplined rehearsals, with every single move, gesture, pause, speech and silence minutely set and plotted.

One of the reasons for this careful plotting is of special interest and has its roots in the audition period. When David Storey happened to see Gerald James audition for Philips for the first time, he felt the whole character of the role to be completely contained in the actor's own personality. The author's intuition was shared by Lindsay Anderson, Anton Gill and Patsy Pollock, the casting director. The only snag was that Gerald James himself did not share their feelings nor their confidence in his ability to play that particular part. After a time, they convinced him and he accepted. During rehearsals, Gerald James' inner conflict grew and the more he thought about the part of Philips and how to play it, the stronger became the conflict. One might say that he was intellectualizing about the part, but this would be to over-simplify and understate the case.

As this inner conflict of Gerald James showed itself during rehearsals in the way he was beginning to play the part, so Lindsay Anderson, David Storey and Anton Gill agreed that the major task was to help him allow the character to spring fully formed from his inner self. The discipline of rehearsals worked and the character of Philips, as well as the particular encounter with Mathews, grew as everyone wanted. During the run, however, Gerald James was still aware of the two concepts (or characters) struggling inside. He said quite openly that it was part of his job as an actor to select what he knew was wanted and to permit only the right things to emerge—no matter how difficult it might be, or what his personal feelings were. David Storey saw the solution as asking Gerald James to put on blinkers to everything except what had been established.

Everyone was content (or as content as one can be in any search for perfection) that the scene was being played the right way—including Gerald James, who spoke with admiration and respect for Lindsay Anderson's sympathetic direction and sensitive rehearsal techniques in *drawing out of him*, not only a good performance, but the *right* one.

Paul Kelly, who played the part of Mathews, had an enlightening comment to make about the particular moment when he first 'finds' the poem he reads aloud. The text is:

MATHEWS (picks up pad: examines other pages. Reads finally):
   'O she was good all right in patches,'

In performance, Philips is busily smoothing a cloth, so fully absorbed, apparently and actually, in what he is doing that he is unaware of Mathews' actions. The discovery of the poem, and Mathews' later speaking it aloud, must take them both unawares. Mathews must come across the poem as if for the first time and Philips must hear it similarly. Provided Philips' absorption is total, his surprise at hearing the words can continue to be real. Gerald James told me that although he knew the gist of the quotations, he deliberately kept the words out of his mind so that his actions, when Mathews stopped speaking on each occasion, continued to be spontaneous. Paul Kelly made the point that in performance he could find the first poem at will (suggesting perhaps that for him they actually existed on the page, which is an interesting idea, since there was no need, from the point of view of the audience, for the words to be there at all, in contrast to the sketches of some of the students' work, which could be seen by the audience fairly easily) but he actually found it when prompted by his intuition, which had been programmed, as it were, by all the previous rhythms and moments in that particular performance. So, in a sense, he too was taken unawares, and even at the apparently technical level of thumb-

ing through the pages of the sketch pad, the 'extra factor' was
still at work.

There are two anecdotes from David Storey that fit well
here since one stems from a line quoted in the passage above.
The line is:

PHILIPS (reads): 'I shall kill Foley . . . Foley is very poorly . . .
    Foley is surely . . .
        the person I shall hourly . . .
        kill . . .
        whenever poor old Allot gets the chance . . .'

The author was approached in a pub near the theatre after
one of the early performances on two separate occasions by
groups who wanted him to confirm or deny their interpretations of the ending of the play. They had in mind specific
things that Allott was going to do after his final exit. The end
of the play is as follows:

FOLEY: A man—if he put his mind to it—can always mend his
    ways. Experience, you see, can put you right . . . In here, the
    mind atrophies, hardens: when the soul is constipated it
    means the nourishment isn't right.
ALLOTT: I'll keep my bowels open.
FOLEY: It'll make a difference, I can tell you that . . . You'll leave
    the life-room tidy? (Waits for ALLOTT's acknowledgement.)
    Set an example, otherwise no one follows. (Puts out his hand.)
    I better say goodnight.
ALLOTT: Goodnight, Principal.

    (Shakes his hand.)
    (FOLEY looks round, briskly: nods: he goes.)
    (ALLOTT looks round: draws on his gloves: pulls up his
    collar: looks round once again, freshly: goes.)

    (FADE.)

Foley: 'I better say goodnight.'
Allott: 'Goodnight Principal.'

What is not mentioned in the text is that the end of the play is accompanied by an upsurge of classical music. This music was an important feature for Lindsay Anderson and will be mentioned again later.

But to return to the groups who had searched out the author in the pub. They were certain that Allott was on his way to do something definite and positive. The first group knew he was going to commit suicide and the second knew he was going to murder Foley. The author's attitude was predictable to a point: that audiences are entitled to think what they will. He was not able to agree that either judgement was in keeping with what he thought his play was about. His explanation of *why* it was important for the groups to decide upon distinct acts for Allott to have in mind was revealing. He suggested that audiences need such pegs on which to hang

their responses so they do not feel lost, and will search to
find them, whether they are there or not. He was concerned
that many people cannot rely on their intuition or feelings
without making for themselves a safety net of narrative. In
particular, he was not pleased that his work had been put into
the category of 'work' plays. Although there may be a point
to such a label the actual labelling tends to obscure the other
qualities of the plays and to call *Life Class* a 'work' play
therefore is to distort it from the beginning. The tragedy here
is that David Storey believes it may be his best play, and,
more significantly, his most poetic. He suggested the hostility
from some audiences and critics can be explained by the fact
that they expected a 'work' play and found something
different. Watching one kind of play, and trying to make it
another, is rather like riding a tiger as if it were a donkey, or
vice versa—a most unpleasant experience either way.

Lindsay Anderson suggested the hostility came from class-
conscious, biased attitudes that saw in *Life Class* the same
challenge as in his film *If*: a threat to Privilege.

It seems true that audiences and critics need pegs of
narrative (the author's or their own) so that absolutely nothing is left unanswered. We should note the words of another
playwright, Ronald Duncan, on plays and poetry alike: 'The
only questions worth asking are those to which there is no
answer.'

There is a well-known sixteenth century saying: 'None so
deaf as those who won't hear.' It is more than relevant to the
incident mentioned above and to the use of music in the
production. Lindsay Anderson raised the question of the
music with me, checking whether or not I had heard it. I was
puzzled at first by his question, since I thought the use of
music to be signal enough not to be missed by anyone. I had
been asked, however, because many people had merely taken

the music as a token that the play had finished—a sign to get ready to leave!

Some modern psychologists maintain that we *can see and hear only what we want to* and this demonstrates clearly how difficult it is for authors, directors and actors to ensure that what they want to say is really understood by the audience. For some, the message will be clear and plain; for many others there will be no message at all, and for others the message will appear to be at odds with what the director wanted. There is no moral here—merely a bald truth about the difficulty of communication, especially in theatre terms. It would appear we have an arduous task in front of us if we are to overcome the situation described by psychologists and perhaps best expressed as 'looking without seeing and listening without hearing'.

And now for all the work that went on before *Life Class* opened at the Royal Court Theatre in April 1974. Early in 1970, David Storey began to write *Life Class*. He wrote the first ten pages or so and then left it completely alone until early in 1973. At that time he was working on another play as well, which took him three days to write.

May 1973: David Storey typed out the script of *Life Class* and, unusually for him, immediately submitted it to Lindsay Anderson. (David Storey recalls only one event between the submission and the December meetings noted below. This was with Lindsay Anderson, in a café in the King's Road: David Storey said, 'Is it worth doing?' Lindsay Anderson replied 'Oh yes.')

4 June 1973: The Artistic Committee of the Royal Court Theatre agreed to present *Life Class*.

25 September 1973: Lindsay Anderson agreed to let the committee know the earliest date by which he could open. The Artistic Director of the Royal Court, Oscar Lewenstein, hoped it would be early April 1974.

30 October 1973: Lindsay Anderson reported that he would be able to open 9 April 1974.

December 1973: Lindsay Anderson and Anton Gill were working together on the transfer of *Farm* to the West End and out of this relationship grew an agreement for them to continue their partnership for *Life Class*.

Before Christmas 1973, preliminary meetings were held between the author, director and director's assistant to discuss production approaches and details. These meetings were followed by discussions with Jocelyn Herbert to talk over details of the stage setting.

Early in January 1974 the crucial task of casting began. Lindsay Anderson insisted on many occasions that this was the most important element in the production; this insistence is logical when we recall his method of working, by exposing the actors' intuitive gifts rather than imposing a rigid formula, which places a greater responsibility on the casting director. For *Life Class* this job was held by Patsy Pollock and it was her first production for the Royal Court.

The method of working was for Anton Gill and Patsy Pollock to draw up long lists of possible actors—especially for the students—and then to pare them down. At this time Alan Bates was sent a copy of the play and gave an early acceptance of the part of Allott.

During the middle of January, Jocelyn Herbert was working on the sketches and models for the first of the set designs.

Towards the end of January, Anton Gill and Patsy Pollock were meeting actors to begin the casting for the students. The auditions at this time were loosely structured and without Lindsay Anderson. This continued for two weeks, with roughly twenty or more actors being seen each day. The auditions were individual and lasted for approximately fifteen minutes each.

During early February, Anton and Patsy were conducting group auditions for the students. In each group there would be eight actors, and each audition would last for an hour with two or three sessions each day.

The set was coming to completion at its model stage. The set builders were beginning to receive instructions and early mention was being made of costume.

Also at this time arrangements were being made for suitable rehearsal rooms (space was important) to be booked.

During the middle of February some student parts had been cast. The final word rested with the director, but he was working in close consultation with his assistant and the casting director, and was always open to suggestions and persuasion. (This is, of course, in keeping with the generous timing schedule for auditions and their informal structure.)

Students at the art school during the performance

At this time the Production Manager was organizing the
stage management crew, and on 21 February there was a full
production team meeting, as shown below:

MEMORANDUM   19th February 1974

TO: Lindsay Anderson

FROM: Peter Wiles (Production Manager)

LIFE CLASS

There will be a Production Meeting for LIFE CLASS
at 5 p.m. on Thursday February 21st in the Production
Office at the Royal Court Theatre (in the hut at the
back of the theatre).

Copies to:		
David Storey	Anton Gill
Jocelyn Herbert	Nick Chelton
Oscar Lewenstein	Juliet Alliston
Knightsbridge Productions	Jenny Tate
Anne Jenkins	John Leonard

Dear Anton,
I hope this is the complete list of people who
should be invited. Is there anyone in connection with
music or sound?
Pete

As they are listed on memorandum, the names refer to the following functions in the production:

Author	Assistant Director
Designer	Lighting Designer
Artistic Director	Company Manager
Partner	Wardrobe Supervisor
General Manager	Master Carpenter

At this time the group auditions were getting fewer and much nearer to final casting. Alan Bates was working with the groups at audition to help promote the right 'feel' as well as expose the *special* qualities being looked for in the parts in question. The Duchess and the Globe theatres were used for the final stage auditions, with Lindsay Anderson and David Storey in attendance.

Some actual set details were also coming along at this time; for example, the donkeys and easels used in art schools for the kind of sketching done in the play. Constant searches had been made for a plaster cast statue but to no avail, and in the actual production one made from fibre glass was used.

By the end of February casting was completed and the understudies were being cast by Anton Gill and Patsy Pollock, with Lindsay Anderson's approval. The set was under construction. Performance work began with a move to the rehearsal rooms.

In the beginning of March the actors were called and the first two weeks were spent in a church hall in Paddington. The first rehearsal was held on the morning of 4 March, and was a straight read-through of the play. In the afternoon of that day the whole cast attended a real life-class with real teachers in a real art school.

The general rehearsal pattern was: 10.30–1.30 and 2.30–6.00 through the week and 1.00–5.00 on Saturdays.

On 5 March and onwards, Act I was rehearsed in detail by Lindsay Anderson and on 9 March Act I was run through.

On 11 March and onwards, Act II was blocked in a similar way to Act I, and on 16 March the whole play was run through.

During the first fortnight the actors were 'on the book' (that is, they had not yet fully learned their lines) but books were completely dispensed with after this period.

Throughout the rehearsal period one basic approach was used: the order of rehearsing scenes was always tied to their order in the play and there was no jumping backwards or forwards within the structure of the play. The overall pattern was: Act I, Act II, Act I, Act II, whole play, and so on.

During the same fortnight the programme was being prepared and the first proofs were delivered by 16 March.

On 18 March the cast began rehearsals in the Royal Court Theatre, getting used to the changes in environment and atmosphere and picking up the threads of the production rhythm.

On 22 March there was the first costume parade with the suggested changes and alterations, and on 23 March the whole play was run through at the Royal Court, without interruption of any kind.

By 25 March the costumes were in order except for one or two specific details, like the street coat worn by Stella, the model, which was given much deliberation before the final choice was made between a new modish coat and a worn one.

During this week the Lighting Designer was watching the rehearsals and the sound tapes were being considered for content, cues and levels, etc. The play was run through fully twice during the week.

On 30 March the play was at a successful run-through

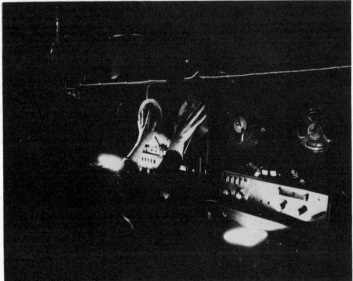

The lighting operators at their desk—just before the performance begins
The tape deck being prepared for performance

LIFE CLASS

PRODUCTION SCHEDULE

SATURDAY MARCH 30th   10.45 pm   Curtain down RUNAWAY

Strike and get-out 'Runaway'

SUNDAY MARCH 31st   Overnight   Complete strike and get-out

Get-in and fit-up LIFE CLASS

4.0 pm   Lighting focussing

9.0 pm   Lighting plotting

MONDAY APRIL 1st   11.0 am   TECHNICAL REHEARSAL (Full Company & Staff
ready to start)

Aft. &   Continuation & Completion of Technical
Evening   Rehearsal

TUESDAY APRIL 2nd   10.0 am   Fire Brigade Scenery Test

Technical work on stage

2.15 pm   DRESS REHEARSAL (Production photos to be
taken by John Haynes)

7.20 pm   FIRST PREVIEW

WEDNESDAY APRIL 3rd   Morning   Technical Work on Stage

Afternoon   Rehearsals to be announced

7.30 pm   SECOND PREVIEW

THURSDAY & FRIDAY   Daytime schedules for rehearsals &
APRIL 4th & 5th   technical work on stage to be announced

PREVIEWS at 7.30 pm

PRESS CALL THURSDAY 12.0 Midday

SATURDAY APRIL 6th   PREVIEWS at 5.0 pm and 8.30 pm

MONDAY APRIL 8th   Rehearsals to be announced
PREVIEW at 7.30 pm

TUESDAY APRIL 9th   Rehearsals to be announced

7.0 pm   PRESS NIGHT - FIRST PERFORMANCE

Subsequent Performances Monday to Friday at 7.30 pm, Saturdays 5.0 pm and
8.30 pm.

Peter Wiles
Production Manager
28.3.74.

stage with the cast at performance level but not at their peak. The actors were sent away for a full week-end break in order to relax and prepare for the last week's production schedule, a facsimile of which appears here. (The only matter not fully covered by it is that, during the preview week, Lindsay Anderson rehearsed bits of the play, watched all performances and gave notes to the cast.)

The designer's sketches shown over page represent Jocelyn Herbert's 'thinking aloud' after reading the script but before meeting any of the cast, since at that time they were still something of an unknown quantity—as the production time-table has shown. The sketches for the setting of the play demonstrate the developments in her mind before she turned to work on a model, and they make a clear statement of her search for the right kind of simplicity and style that eventually appeared on the stage.

The sketches for the costumes represent her response to the text, and it is a token of her special talent and flair that, in the main, they accurately reflect what suited the actors best when it came to choosing their individual costumes during re-hearsal. This was confirmed by the fact that Jocelyn Herbert actually found many of the stage costumes she wanted among each actor's personal clothing. When this occurred, as it did particularly with the students, the clothes were then bought for the production.

The rest of the chapter is given over to sketches, pictures and documentation from the production, showing some, at least, of the many roads taken.

Anton Gill to Derek Bowskill

'I will try to describe what I felt like during the production of *Life Class*, but it will be a difficult job because most of the time I was too busy or too tired to feel more than the most

MATHEWS

ALLOTT

FOLEY

PHILLIPS

basic relief, irritation, interest, elation and boredom. The
keenest emotion without doubt is what one feels as the curtain
goes up on the First Night and that is always the same: relief
that it's all out of one's hands, trepidation about what the
critics will say (although as an Assistant Director this particular feeling isn't very keen) and a curious sense of loss. All
the panic and insane rush of the week leading up to this one
particular evening are dissolved instantly. There is suddenly
nothing to do and one goes to bed that night feeling pole-axed
and rather sad.

'Having started, then, at the end, I'll go back to the
beginning. It helps if you like the play. There's nothing worse
than working on a play in which you have no faith, especially
as you aren't going to have the opportunity of shaping the
play artistically, only of looking after it and making sure the
Director has a happy delivery, and on time. It also helps if
you get on with the Director and agree with his ideas, because
you'll only feel frustrated if you don't. I have always been
lucky in these two respects. I've never disliked a director
(although there are always times when you and he could
happily kill each other) and I've only twice worked on a play
which has struck me as unworthy of production. All right,
you like the play, you like the Director, so you feel enthusiastic and ready to do your damndest to get the production on
the road. This isn't boy-scout enthusiasm; it's something
you've got to have if you're going to find the necessary energy
to see you through your work for the next three months,
when you will actually be frustrated and bored more often
than you will be on top. The best feeling you will usually get
is relief: relief that the Director likes the rehearsal room you
have sweated blood hiring, relief that the actors are a decent
bunch and aren't going to upset the stage management by
ordering special brands of instant coffee to drink in their

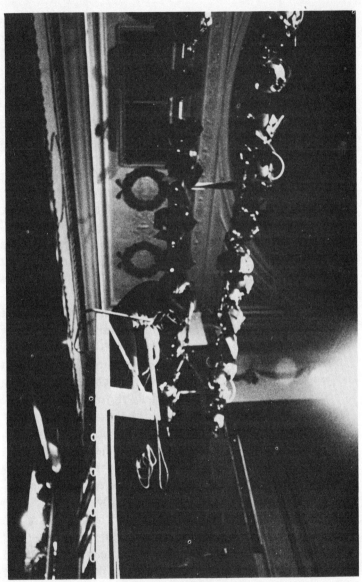

High above the auditorium, an electrician makes final adjustments
before the performance

breaks, relief that the Director doesn't send you off on errands all over London which keep you away from watching the play evolve in rehearsal. You will also feel irritated when all these things do happen. Provided, however, that you have basic faith in the play, you will be all right and all your suffering will be transitory. It's fatal to let anything get on top of you for long, since the minute one thing gets there another will, and it'll become increasingly difficult to emerge from the mess.

'The next thing you feel is worry. Will the leading actor's newspaper interview (arranged by you and the Press Office) upset him when it appears? If so, who will get the stick? You or the Press Office? Usually, directors are quite fair in handing out stick but in the sheer nervous tension generated by a production in rehearsal it's forgivable if the innocent get hit sometimes! You also worry about everything from the ASM's poor coffee-making to the programme copy, from the sound-effects tape to an understudy's toothache. Usually you are a fool to worry because everything, finally and somehow, resolves itself, but you worry anyway. At its worst, this worry can keep you remorselessly on the edge of sleep all night while angry directors and unlikely props chase you through hideous mazes until dawn, especially if you've been at the Scotch all the previous evening.

'I'd better say a little about the good things you feel. Again, they have a lot to do with your attitude to the play. Curiously, your attitude to the play is more important than your attitude to the actors or even the Director. If you really like the play then nothing demanded of you by anybody else involved in its production will seem unreasonable. The quality of the play will provide a constant stimulus and the only thing you will hate is when you have to leave the rehearsal room on some errand or other. The play leads, the rest follows. Next

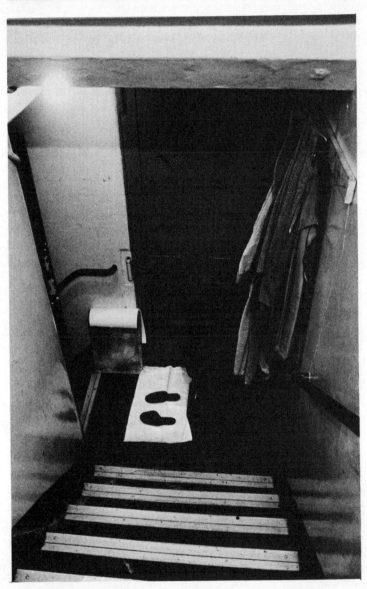

Back-stage: one of the many small preparations for performance

in importance is the Director's attitude to the play. If he is doing what you might do, then it is pleasing to see and learn from how he does it. If his attitude differs from yours, you can still learn (possibly more) if you think he's a good director. To me, learning is always a pleasure; it is also *the* important thing an assistant director can get from his job. Next in importance is probably the director's attitude to you. Here, it's a much simpler matter. If he clearly likes you, consults you, makes you feel as if you were rather more than a useful but often irritating errand-boy, you are bound to feel happier. I have nearly always been lucky, as I've already said, so my basic feeling has nearly always been one of happy involvement. I would say that without this feeling one should give up, but it's rare not to achieve it.

'Frustration is one's worst enemy. An assistant director in the theatre isn't making a career of being an assistant director. He is serving a kind of informal apprenticeship, a grub trying to become a butterfly himself. If he stays a grub too long, either out of laziness or bad luck, and doesn't start directing plays himself, he becomes frustrated. In any job frustration is *the* emasculator and in the theatre its victims are legion. I have assisted on five shows now and that's really too many. It's very easy to become lulled into a false sense of security once one has learnt to do the job well, and one can find oneself thinking that the job is an important one. It isn't really. In most theatres, the assistant's job is shared by the Stage Manager and the Director. It's not a profession in itself. It's a transient period, very valuable, but a fatal groove in which to stick. Fortunately, the theatre is so structured that the likelihood of sticking is slight.

'As an Assistant Director you belong to none of the groups involved in a production, by which I mean the actors, the stage management and the Director. Thus you do tend to feel

lonely sometimes, but on the other hand, most of the time you
don't have the leisure to feel lonely.

'I could go on and tell you how it feels when you're doing
understudy rehearsals and suddenly discover that two of the
understudies aren't talking to each other, or about what goes
through your mind when an actor hasn't appeared by the half
and the understudy on standby is fainting in your arms, but
I won't. You can imagine it! Instead, as I'm sure I've said
enough, I'll just wish any prospective Assistant "Good Luck"
and stop.'

On-stage: relaxing and preparing for the performance

Off-stage: the cast of *Life Class*

[Handwritten manuscript notes reproduced in typeset form below:]

LIFE CLASS.
ACT ONE

A *[illegible]* stage.

Off-centre, *[illegible]*, is a wooden platform, on castors. *[illegible]*

Beside it *[crossed out]* is a *[illegible]* metal stand, equipped with two vertical flat-plate heater.

Scattered around the platform are several wooden 'donkeys': *[illegible]* low, flat stools with an upright T shaped bar at one end. On one, folded, is a white sheet.

There are two *[illegible]* screens, *[illegible]* the other *[illegible]* left, and a rack with coatpegs.

ALLOTT comes in *[illegible]*.

Shivers.

[crossed out]

[illegible] he *[illegible]* wear a duffle-coat, *[battered trilby hat]* *[illegible]* gloves.

[crossed out]

Blows in his hands. Thumps gloves:

Shivers.

Looks round.

                        ACT ONE

A stage.

Off-centre, stage-right, is a wooden platform, some six to
eight feet square, on castors.

Beside it are two metal stands, about six feet high, each
equipped with two vertical flat-plate heaters.

Scattered around the platform are several wooden 'donkeys':
low, rectangular stools with an upright T shaped bar at
one end. On one, folded, is a white sheet.

There are two brown hessian screens, one upstage centre,
the other centre left. Upstage left is a rack with coatpegs.

ALLOTT comes in stage-left.

In his late thirties, medium-build, he wears a duffle-coat,
battered trilby hat, and gloves.

Blows in his hands. Thumps gloves.

Shivers.

Looks round.

To throne break L.
X to DR (on lights)
to Centre R. above
throne to lectern X to
L lectern break for L
behind lectern
X to throne O. to R.   (O = "round")

WARREN: ①   'Morning, sir.

ALLOTT: 'Morning, Warren. ②

                    ✓ (WARREN watches ALLOTT a while,
                        adjusting platform)

WARREN: ... Nobody else here then, yet, Mr. Allott.

ALLOTT: ③ Perfectly correct. (pays WARREN no attention)

WARREN: Er ... cold.

ALLOTT: Very.

WARREN: Get a cup of tea.

ALLOTT: That's right.

WARREN: Well ... See you.

ALLOTT: ④ Hope so.

WARREN: ⑤ Yeh. (last look round: he goes)

                    (ALLOTT steps back: contemplates.
                ✓ Goes over to heater: carries it round
                    to the platform's new position.

                    SAUNDERS comes in: thin, anaemic:
                    raincoat, young)

SAUNDERS: 'Morning, sir.

ALLOTT: Saunders.

SAUNDERS: ⑥   Need any help, sir?

ALLOTT: Let's see. ⑦ (takes off gloves: takes off coat)
           Could hang that up somewhere. (then hat)
           And that.

SAUNDERS: Right. (takes them)

ALLOTT: Er ... Over there, I think ⑧ ... That's right ...
           Now, then. Chalk. Pencil ⑨ (feels in jacket
           pockets: checks) Toilet paper ... Seen Mr.
           Philips, have you?

SAUNDERS: ⑩   No, sir.

① *illegible* x below to L.

② *illegible* go U/S

③ Saunder D/L to centre ? x U/S to *illegible* begin *illegible*.
→ Round to R at *illegible*

④ Stella to L. lecker

⑤ Saunders takes tray.

Saunders: coat off on pegs. ←

Saunders *illegible* his *illegible*, changes his stuff on it, then walks platform.

ALLOTT: Had some unfinished business there, I recollect.

SAUNDERS: Anything else, sir?

ALLOTT: No ... Yes. Could chalk the platform. There's a lad. (hands him chalk)

SAUNDERS: Right.

ALLOTT: Shan't be a sec ... (hesitates. Looks round) ...Right. (he goes)

 (SAUNDERS chalks off the corners of the platform on the floor.

As he reaches the ~~third~~ second corner STELLA comes in: a model, in her twenties: she's muffled up in a heavy coat and cap: carries a shopping-bag as well as a handbag)

STELLA: Freezing. (shivers: [goes directly to the heater])

SAUNDERS: Just setting this ...

STELLA: Mr. Allott here?

SAUNDERS: He's just gone out ...

STELLA: You wouldn't pop these in the cubicle, would you, love?

SAUNDERS: Yes. (takes the bag and handbag)

STELLA: Do my shopping on the way up. Get in early ... Worth all the trouble ... I'll be in the ... Shan't be long.

(She goes: SAUNDERS crosses to the upstage screen: takes bags behind.

Pause.

MATHEWS comes in: he's followed by BRENDA.

MATHEWS wears a windcheater. He's smoking. BRENDA wears a coat: both are young.

MATHEWS drops his cigarette, treads it out.)

THE ROYAL COURT THEATRE
AND EDDIE KULUKUNDIS PRESENT

Alan Bates
in
**LIFE
CLASS**
by
David Storey

directed by
Lindsay Anderson

designed by
Jocelyn Herbert
lighting by
Nick Chelton

Stephen Bent
Brenda Cavendish
Brian Glover
Frank Grimes
Gerald James
Paul Kelly

David Lincoln
Gabrielle Lloyd
Rosemary Martin
Bob Peck
Stuart Rayner
Sally Watts

**ROYAL
COURT
THEATRE**
Sloane Square SW1
01·730 1745

8 YOUNG PEOPLE'S THEATRE

THE FIRST POINT TO BE NOTED about Theatre for Young People is that most of it is run *for* young people and not *by* young people. The upper age limit for this section of theatre is 21, so readers under this please do something about it: take your kind of theatre into your hands and do with it what you want to do. Only then will there be a real hope that the theatre of tomorrow will not be a tarnished reflection of yesterday. Older people are not necessarily wiser and in any artistic activity are more likely to be unexperimental and rigid.

The second point of note is that Theatre for Young People (often referred to as TYP) has only been around in this country for thirty years and the first twenty were slow in development. The last decade, however, has shown a mushrooming, due in large part to the distribution of funds by the Arts Council of Great Britain.

There are four main categories of theatre for young people and many of them overlap, but, for the sake of clarity, they are presented here as separate entities.

1. Groups of adults who observe, oversee and supervise: Local Education Authorities; The Arts Council of Great Britain; Regional and Local Arts Councils; and the National

Council of Theatre For Young People. The objects and membership of this last-mentioned body are given below.

Objects

To advance the education of young people through the theatre and dramatic arts and to foster and encourage such development by the co-ordination, correlation and development of all aspects of theatre·for young people. In furtherance of the above, but not otherwise:

(a) to provide guidance, information and other assistance to organizations and persons working in the field of theatre for young people;

(b) to arrange for the collection, collation and dissemination of information in the field of theatre for young people;

(c) to consult and co-operate with, or make representations to central and local government departments and international, national and local organizations;

(d) to receive, hold, administer and raise funds for the use of the objects of the Council;

(e) to engage in other activities directly necessary to the attainments of the primary objects of the Council.

Membership

Membership of the Council shall consist of the Officers elected by the Council and two representatives of each of the following non-profit distributing bodies:

British Children's Theatre Association
Council of Regional Theatres
Educational Drama Association
Young Theatre Association
National Association of Drama Advisers
Puppet Theatre Centre Committee
National Youth Theatre
Society of Authors
Society of Teachers of Speech and Drama

Association of Teachers in Colleges and
Departments of Education—Drama Section

Other non-profit distributing bodies may be invited by the Council
to become members, subject to the approval of a majority of the
members of the Council.

2. Groups of adults who perform *to and for* young people.
There are hundreds of groups in this category and the
variety is vast: from amateur to professional; from very large
to very small; and from permanent to once-only ventures.
The Young Vic is known internationally as well as at home
and is, in many ways, the symbol of the current interest in
Theatre for Young People.

The National Theatre at the Young Vic
The Young Vic, under its director Frank Dunlop, is part of the
National Theatre of Great Britain.

In an interview in February 1969 Sir Laurence Olivier talked
of '. . . the plan for a new experimental venture as part of the
National—a new temporary building in The New Cut close by the
Old Vic . . . This is really Frank's baby . . . We call it the Young
Vic in affectionate memory of George Devine. Here we think to
develop plays for young audiences, an experimental workshop for
authors, actors and producers; a kind of Old Vic in which I, and
all my generation, were able to cut our teeth on the big classic
roles without being too harshly judged for it . . .'

The National Theatre put its first scheme to the Arts Council of
Great Britain for a Young People's Theatre Centre in February
1968.

The plan was to erect a temporary building with performance
space for large presentations to about 450–500 people and experimental work. It was to be a Centre for work of a national standard
to be available to students and young people whose incomes or
inclinations make existing theatre expensive or forbidding, and
would include the basic classics, providing education in theatre;
plays specially written for young people; experimental theatre

work; music (from the more popular to the classics), fine arts, films, etc. It was to be a kind of open university of the arts and a firework display to provoke the imagination.

Work began on 2 September 1969, and the Theatre was declared open by Dame Sybil Thorndike on 12 August 1970. The first performance to the public took place on 15 September 1970, and was *Scapino*, based on Molière's 'Les Fourberies de Scapi'. The Press acclaimed both the production and the Theatre.

3. Groups of adults who perform mainly *with* young people, often under the title of 'audience participation'. The variety here is just as vast as in the second category, though the numbers are smaller. Some have permanent homes and some are without; some are attached to base theatres and some exist in isolation; and some use writers and some create their own programmes. The following notes of some of the work of the Theatre-in-Education Company (many are known as T.I.E.'s) of the Octagon Theatre, Bolton, give a taste of the kind of work undertaken by such groups.

The Theatre-in-Education Company is financed by the Arts Council of Great Britain and Bolton Education Authority. Members are specifically appointed to the T.I.E. Company to combine their teaching techniques and their theatre skills to create a learning situation. The Company operates in local primary and secondary schools, youth clubs and colleges of further education.

'Spy Ring', for one class of eight-year-old children. Spy Ring is a half-day programme taking place in and around the school. During the story, the children have to make two decisions: (1) which of three brothers is most reliable, and (2) should an eccentric old lady be evicted from the caravan.

'The Betrayal of the Aztecs', for ten-year-olds. In the picture, Spaniards and Tlaxcalans witness the conversion by Captain Cortes of Montezuma to Christianity. Behind them, they suspect that the Aztecs are spying, fearing that the emperor might be betraying his own Aztec religion.

'Blood, Sweat and Tears', for one class of fourth or fifth form pupils. Grouped round tables, the pupils watch a series of scenes about young people's problems. The group then refers to project books and discusses, together with the characters, before answering the questions.

'Gremian', a programme for one class of six- and seven-year-old children. In the story, the children help the Gremians. They 'travel' in their dome from rubbish dump to rubbish dump in their battle against the Burks.

'Dollar Bill's U.S.A. Show', a youth club play. The Company tour youth clubs with specially written or chosen plays. Other activities for young people in their leisure time include a weekly drama club at the studio, holiday courses, street theatre and youth leaders' courses.

'John Chamberlain & Co. Ltd.', a programme for sixth form pupils. The pupils assume the roles of union members, supervisors and managers, and experience some of the conflicts at a car factory when the Industrial Relations Act is implemented.

4. Groups of adults who sponsor or promote classes or productions for young people. These vary from professional, nationally based organizations to informal, local amateur groups. Local Education Authority Drama Advisers are playing an increasingly important part in this category, especially in the areas of drama classes, theatre workshops, improvisation and dance-drama groups. Working in a different way is the National Youth Theatre under its director and initiator, Michael Croft.

The following statement comes from the Secretary of the National Association of Drama Advisers, and is of particular interest to those who wish to try drama for themselves.

Youth Drama
Those who have enjoyed and developed an interest in drama work during their secondary school careers are often faced with a

problem when they leave if they wish to pursue this interest. It is certainly true to say that more drama work of all kinds is being undertaken in secondary schools today than at any time in the past, and consequently more young people will be looking for outlets when they leave.

For the person who wishes to practise drama as an amateur, two basic choices exist: working with adults or working with contemporaries. The former normally involves joining one of the many amateur dramatic societies which abound throughout the country. Whether or not such a move would be a wise one depends on several factors, including the quality of the society's work and organization as well as its attitude towards its younger members, but a common drawback is the lack of scope for those interested in acting or production. Teenagers in most societies of this kind are restricted to teenage roles. No producer is going to cast a young member in a middle-aged part when he has an actor of this age available. Similarly, most societies will not allow anyone to direct a play until he or she has gained a few years experience.

It seems to me therefore that it is best to avoid this kind of restriction and to join a group of young people. Some of the larger, well-established amateur societies possess a separate section for young members, but these are few and far between. Some Youth Centres possess enthusiastic and enterprising drama groups, but these often have to contend with difficult working conditions and a lack of suitable facilities, especially in the open plan centres.

Perhaps the most encouraging development over the past few years has been the increasing provision by Local Education Authorities of Youth Theatre Workshops, many of them operating in fully equipped drama studios or centres under the direction of trained drama specialists. Whether or not these workshops concern themselves with scripted plays or improvised group-created theatre, the scope and the opportunity to experiment are limitless. Most of the amateur societies tend to be reluctant to experiment with new forms, which is a pity when one realizes that the full potential of theatre has yet to be exploited and that the time that the profession can devote to this end is limited. On the other hand, a great deal of experimental work has emerged from the Youth Theatre Workshops, which have produced some of the most exciting theatre that I have seen in recent years.

Most counties possess such workshops, although their locations may not be generally known. Specific information about them can be obtained from the County Drama Adviser for the area concerned. He or she will also be able to provide information on drama courses for youth, for which most education authorities make a generous provision.

It is true to say that the needs of most young people can nowadays be met, whatever particular form of drama they wish to pursue. It is not within the scope of this article to write in detail about the avenues open to the minority who wish to enter the theatre profession. These will of course require full-time training, and here again it is important that they consult their County Drama Adviser before making any final decisions. Advice on the most appropriate course and the possibilities of grant aid is essential to anyone wishing to embark on theatre as a career. The same applies to those wishing to train as teachers of drama. The County Drama Adviser can be contacted through the Local Education Office.

John Boylan, Senior Adviser for Drama, Cambridgeshire

In his interesting book *The National Youth Theatre*, Simon Masters introduces it as follows: 'The National Youth Theatre was founded by Michael Croft (in 1956) from a group of schoolboy actors: it has grown into a national organization staging anything up to seven productions a year in London's West End, the Provinces and on the Continent— all during school holidays—and it has set a new standard in youth drama, being acclaimed year after year by the critics for the all-round excellence of its productions. At times, indeed, critics have observed that productions deserve to outrun long established West End successes.

'It has been variously described as "an entirely satisfactory and rewarding Way of Life", and "an indoor Outward Bound Course minus fresh air and sleep". For its members it offers an experience so great that their lives cannot help being broadened and enriched.'

The National Youth Theatre

Since its inception in 1956, over 4,000 young people have taken part in National Youth Theatre productions and drama courses. They have come from schools and colleges throughout the country. The only qualification is that of age: all applicants must be aged between 14 and 21.

Members are not recruited from universities, drama schools or the professional theatre—although those who join the NYT while they are still at school are allowed to remain in the company to the upper age limit should they become full-time students.

Members have to pay the cost of travel and subsistence during the weeks they are in London. The NYT cannot provide hostel accommodation but tries to give assistance and advice with regard to hostels and suitable lodgings. The annual season takes place in August and September. Acting members are usually based at Haverstock School, Chalk Farm, NW1, for the rehearsal period and thereafter either at the Shaw Theatre or another theatre in north London. Technical members are based at the NYT Workshops, West London Docks, London, E1.

NYT members are eligible for grants towards the costs of travel and subsistence from the Local Authorities. The national average is 50 per cent of total costs, although some LEA's pay less than one-third of total costs, and a few still contribute nothing at all.

The NYT provides adult supervision in every department of production but members are encouraged to develop qualities of initiative and self-dependence. Out of working hours they are expected to look after themselves and to gain the maximum educational and social benefit from their stay in London.

Actors are selected on the basis of audition and interview, although the formal audition is by no means all-important. A good audition may prove very little and vice versa. Applicants are often accepted who do a hopeless audition but show unusual or interesting qualities—or even a need to be helped—in their interview. No method of selection is perfect and inevitably many deserving candidates are turned down; but each year the maximum possible number is accepted for all departments of production. Every applicant is given an interview and nobody should be deterred from applying through lack of experience or any feeling of inferiority or unsuitability.

The National Youth Theatre is grant-aided by the Arts Council, the Department of Education and Science and King George's Jubilee Trust. The NYT's past successes include a modern dress production of *Julius Caesar*, first performed in 1961, and the first performances of several plays by Peter Terson, notably *Zigger Zagger*, *The Apprentices* and *Good Lads at Heart*.

In 1965, the National Youth Theatre became the only amateur company to be invited to perform at the Old Vic, with highly acclaimed productions of *Antony and Cleopatra* and *Troilus and Cressida*. The NYT has represented Great Britain at the International Festivals of Berlin (three times), Holland (twice), and the Theatre des Nations in Paris.

SOME GIANTS
OF THE THEATRE

AESCHYLUS (525–456 B.C.), the father of Greek drama. He was a gifted poet and courageous soldier, born near Athens and died in Sicily. It is said he wrote more than ninety plays and the titles of more than seventy are known although only seven are available to us. He gained many victories and prizes in the fiercely competitive Greek Drama Festivals. He set a shining example for important Greek playwrights who followed him—Sophocles, Euripides and Aristophanes. His only serious rival in 2,500 years has been Shakespeare. Legend has it that he was killed by a tortoise falling on his head, released by a passing eagle that mistook his bald head for a stone.

ARTAUD, Antonin (1896–1948), French poet, actor, director, writer, playwright and innovator. His genius appealed to few during his lifetime and many dismissed him as lunatic. His most influential published work is *Le Théatre et son double*, and his impact has been widespread since his death, dramatically changing the direction of European plays and their staging.

BECKETT, Samuel (1906–   ), Irish poet/novelist/dramatist who has lived mainly in Paris and written in French. His best known play is *Waiting for Godot* and his influence upon contemporary writers, directors and actors has been profound. The depth and breadth of his concept of the human condition, coupled with his command of theatre skills and his compelling, poetic use of language, entitle him to be placed on a par with Shakespeare.

BERNHARDT, Sarah (1845–1923), a world-famous French actress with an outstanding talent for professional flair and personal temperament, and equally outstanding beauty of voice and figure. She became in her lifetime the archetype 'great actress', and no one has really succeeded her in that image.

BRECHT, Bertolt (1898–1956), German poet/playwright/director/ critic/teacher who sought to remove all elements of sloppy thinking and illusion from the theatre. He failed (but brilliantly so) to put his ideas into his plays. His achievement lies in what other writers and directors gained from his ideas and productions, and his impact, in a completely different direction, is equal to that of Artaud.

CRAIG, Gordon (1872–1966), an English child actor who turned to scenic design as the only hope for a theatre that he despised. His ideas were startlingly original and abundant, and the theatre today is still coming to terms with many of them. His influence has been tremendous, but it did not show itself in the way, or at the time, that Craig needed and he became a recluse.

IBSEN, Henrik (1828–1906), Norwegian playwright who changed the direction of European and American drama. The range of his work is vast, but his major contribution lies in his total re-jigging of the sentimental, unthinking theatre of his day. He was the first dramatist to succeed in presenting the thoughts, feelings, problems, obsessions, hopes and fears of the ordinary people of his own times in a credible manner. That he did so with poetic skill, theatrical expertise and great passion is a tribute to his unique gifts.

IRVING, Sir Henry (1838–1905), an English actor-manager who did for men what Bernhardt did for women. He started acting as an amateur and rose to dominate the London stage. His fame was international and he was the first actor to be knighted for his services to the theatre.

LITTLEWOOD, Joan (1914–   ), an English director and innovator who picked her private path through the works of Artaud, Brecht and Stanislavsky to create a stamp of her own: the idea of a co-operative, people's theatre. She is best known for her work at the Theatre Royal, Stratford, London, and as the founder of Theatre Workshop in the north of England in 1945. Her main successes still defeat her wish to change the nature of the commercial theatre, a piece of dramatic irony she is the first to recognize.

MARLOWE, Christopher (1564–?), an English playwright who made a major contribution to the Elizabethan theatre. He was a controversial figure involved in much womanizing, drinking, fighting and spying. His religious and political views placed him well in advance of his times and his spying merely contributed to making him an apparent danger to the State. It is possible he rigged his apparent assassination to enable him to continue writing, and some believe that he was the author of Shakespeare's plays.

MOLIÈRE (1622–73), French actor and playwright whose works approach the stature of Shakespeare and who is undoubtedly one of the greatest French dramatists. He brought a delicacy of touch and nicety of language to the style of the commedia dell'arte (in which area he first started work) and raised comedy to a peak. He has not been well served in translation but has, in spite of this, achieved marked popularity in England.

OLIVIER, Sir Laurence (1907–   ), English actor and director in direct line with the tradition of Irving, but with a wide versatility and insight. He virtually established the National Theatre Company at a stroke, and the National Theatre on the South Bank will be his effective monument.

SHAKESPEARE, William (1564–1616), a perfect example of the

right man, in the right place, at the right time. He brought to miraculous bloom the theatre of his day and has been root, tree, branch and limb ever since. He is living proof of the untruth that 'you can't please all the people all the time'. He did, does and will continue to do so.

STANISLAVSKY, Constantin (1863–1938), Russian actor/director/ teacher who did for theatre production what Ibsen did for writing. His main contribution was to insist on the importance, not of what was done or said (in real life or on the stage), but of what was meant. It is a fitting tribute that his work became known as the 'Stanislavsky method', now universally acknowledged by the approach to theatre training and production acclaimed as 'Method'.

ORGANIZATIONS AND SUPPLIERS

Organizations

Arts Council of Great Britain, 105 Piccadilly, London, W1V 0AU.

British Amateur Drama Association, Orbis, Youlgrave, Nr. Bakewell, Derbyshire.

British Children's Theatre Association, c/o British Theatre Association.

British Theatre Association, 9–10 Fitzroy Square, London W1P 6AE.

Drama Board, 20 Beaumont Street, Oxford, OX1 2NQ.

Educational Drama Association, Drama Centre, Rea Street, Birmingham, 5.

Guild of Drama Adjudicators, 26 Bedford Square, London, WC1B 3HU.

National Drama Conference, 26 Bedford Square, London, WC1B 3HU.

Radius, Religious Drama Society of Great Britain, George Bell House, Bishop's Hall, Ayres Street, London, SE1.

Scottish Arts Council, 11 Rothesay Terrace, Edinburgh, 3.

Scottish Community Drama Association, 78 Queen Street, Edinburgh, 2.

Society of Teachers of Speech & Drama, 82 St. John's Road, Sevenoaks, Kent.

Welsh Arts Council, 9 Museum Place, Cardiff, CF1 3NX.

Young Theatre Association, c/o British Theatre Association.

The following may all be contacted at the British Theatre Association:

Association of British Theatre Technicians.
British Children's Theatre Association.
Little Theatre Guild of Great Britain.
National Association of Drama Advisers.
National Council of Theatre for Young People.
Society of Theatre Consultants.
Theatres' Advisory Council.

Suppliers
The following are major suppliers in their own field:

Books, plays, acting editions, sound effects and play guides:
Samuel French Ltd., 26 Southampton Street, Strand, London, WC2.
Make-up, costumes, wigs and properties:
Charles Fox Ltd., 25 Shelton Street, London WC2H 9HX.
Stage lighting:
W. J. Furse & Co. Ltd., Traffic Street, Nottingham, NG2 1NF.
Rank Strand Electric Ltd., PO Box 70, Great West Road, Brentford, Middlesex, TW8 9HR.

FURTHER READING

Reading Lists

Brochures available from Stacey Publications, 1 Hawthorndene Road, Bromley, Kent, include the following:

Stage Make-up
Your Problems Solved
The Play Produced
Stage Lighting for Clubs and Schools
Plays of 1966 onwards (separate annual publications)
Theatre Directory (a comprehensive guide to services, suppliers and organizations)

Regular Publications

Amateur Stage (monthly, Stacey Publications)
British Theatre Directory (annually, 1 Susans Road, Eastbourne)
Drama (quarterly, British Theatre Association)
Plays and Players (monthly, 75 Victoria Street, London, SW1)
Stage and Television Today (weekly, 19/21 Tavistock Street, London, WC2)
Theatre Quarterly (ABP Ltd., North Way, Andover Way, Hants.)

Books

Artaud, Antonin, *The Theatre and its Double*, Calder & Boyars, London, 1970.
Bentley, Eric, *The Theatre of Commitment*, Methuen, London, 1968.
      What is Theatre?, Methuen, London, 1969.

Bowskill, Derek, *Acting and Stagecraft Made Simple*, W. H. Allen, London, 1973.

Drama and the Teacher, Pitman Publishing, London, 1974.

Brustein, Robert, *The Theatre of Revolt*, Methuen, London, 1970.

Burton, Peter, and Lane, John, *New Directions*, Methuen, London, 1972.

Clark, Brian, *Group Theatre*, Pitman Publishing, London, 1971.

Esslin, Martin, *The Theatre of the Absurd*, Penguin, London, 1970.

Grotowski, Jerzy, *Towards a Poor Theatre*, Methuen, London, 1969.

Hartnoll, Phyllis (Ed.), *The Concise Oxford Companion to the Theatre*, Oxford University Press, London, 1972.

Joseph, Stephen, *New Theatre Forms*, Pitman Publishing, London, 1968.

Pronko, Leonard, *Avant Garde: The Experimental Theatre in France*, Cambridge University Press, London, 1962.

Stanislavsky, Constantin, *Building a Character*, Methuen, London, 1968.

Williams, Raymond, *Drama in Performance*, Penguin, London, 1972.

Drama from Ibsen to Brecht, Chatto & Windus, London, 1968.

The following more specialized titles are all available from Studio Vista, London.

Angeloglou, Maggie, *A History of Make-up*, 1970.

Cunnington, Phillis, *Costume in Pictures*, 1964.

Evans, James Roose, *Experimental Theatre*, 1970.

Hobbs, William, *Techniques of the Stage Fight*, 1967.

Jackson, Sheila, *Simple Stage Costumes*, 1964.

Motley, *Designing and Making Stage Costumes*, 1968.

Percival, John, *Modern Ballet*, 1970.

Pilbrow, Richard, *Stage Lighting*, 1971.

Warre, Michael, *Designing and Making Stage Scenery*, 1966.

TRAINING

A career in the theatre has always been tempting to many young people and problematic for many of them. But if you have any talent at all and refuse to take 'no' for an answer, you should manage to find work. Opportunities are better now than ever before, so do not be put off by the mystique (that is only a cover-up for the untalented) nor wrongly tempted by the glamour, but pursue your real theatre for all that it is worth. A healthy society requires a vigorous theatre to keep it so.

There is little doubt that the best way into the theatre is through a drama school. The following list contains the major schools in the country but does not refer to university drama departments, of which there are now a number.

Actor's Forum, 64 Evelyn Avenue, London, NW9 0JH.

Actor's Workshop, 124 Polesworth House, Alfred Road, London, W2 5HD.

Arts Educational School, Golden Lane House, Golden Lane, London, EC1.

Birmingham School of Speech Training and Dramatic Art, 45 Church Road, Edgbaston, Birmingham, B15 2NE.

Birmingham Theatre School, Station Street, Birmingham.

Bristol Old Vic Theatre School, 2 Downside Road, Bristol, BS8 2XF.

Burton School of Speech and Drama, Guild Street, Burton-on-Trent, Staffs., DE15 0JN.

Central School of Speech and Drama, Embassy Theatre, Eton Avenue, London, NW3 3HY.

Corona Stage School, 16 Ravenscourt Avenue, London, W6 0SL.

Dance Centre Limited, 12 Floral Street, London, WC2.

Drama Centre Limited, 176 Prince of Wales Road, Chalk Farm, London, NW5 3PT.

East 15 Acting School, 'Hatfields', Rectory Lane, Loughton, Essex.

Guildhall School of Music and Drama, John Carpenter Street, Victoria Embankment, London EC4Y 0AR.

London Academy of Music and Dramatic Art, 226 Cromwell Road, London, SW5.

London School of Dramatic Art, 14 Glentworth Street, London, NW1.

London Opera Centre, 490 Commercial Road, London, E1 0HX.

New College of Speech and Drama, Ivy House, North End Road, London, NW11.

Rose Bruford Training College of Speech and Drama, Lamorbey Park, Sidcup, Kent.

Royal Academy of Dancing, 48 Vicarage Crescent, London, SW11 3LT.

Royal Academy of Dramatic Art, 62/4 Gower Street, London, WC1.

Royal Ballet School, 155 Talgarth Road, London, W14.

Royal Scottish Academy of Music and Drama, St. George's Place, Glasgow, G2 1BS.

Webber Douglas Academy of Dramatic Art, 30/36 Clareville Street, London, SW7.

Welsh College of Music and Drama, The Castle, Cardiff, CF1 2RB.

There are also many universities, colleges of education and further education that run full and part-time courses in drama and theatre. Details of many of these may be found in the *British Theatre Directory*, published annually by Vance-Offord Ltd., Eastbourne.

INDEX